BEAUTIFUL BEADED
JEWELRY
FOR BEGINNERS

25 Rings, Bracelets, Necklaces, and Other Step-by-Step Projects

CHERYL OWEN

Published 2018—IMM Lifestyle Books
www.IMMLifestyleBooks.com

IMM Lifestyle Books are distributed in the UK by Grantham Book Service, Trent Road, Grantham, Lincolnshire, NG31 7XQ.

In North America, IMM Lifestyle Books are distributed by Fox Chapel Publishing, 903 Square Street, Mount Joy, PA 17552, *www.FoxChapelPublishing.com.*

All photography by Paul Bricknell (Paul Bricknell Photography Ltd) except Shutterstock photos as follows: page 2: Melanina Evgeniya; pages 4–5 and 136 (background): Denis Ulyanov; page 9: Prostock-studio; pages 24–25: Melanina Evgeniya; page 30 (bottom left): Ira Shpiller; page 38 (top left): Volodymyr Nikitenko; page 46 (left): Riabchynskaia; page 66 (bottom left): bjphotographs; page 84 (bottom left): Melanina Evgeniya; page 94 (bottom): Natasha Breen; page 104 (bottom left): Tamara Kulikova; page 108 (bottom left): mahmood alishahi; page 131 (bottom right): Ekaterina Shakhova.

ISBN 978-1-5048-0107-2

Library of Congress Cataloging-in-Publication Data

Names: Owen, Cheryl, author.
Title: Beautiful beaded jewelry for beginners / Cheryl Owen.
Description: Mount Joy, PA : IMM Lifestyle Books, 2018. | Includes index.
Identifiers: LCCN 2018012323 | ISBN 9781504801072 (pbk.)
Subjects: LCSH: Beadwork. | Jewelry making.
Classification: LCC TT860 .O9424 2018 | DDC 745.594/2--dc23
LC record available at https://lccn.loc.gov/2018012323

We are always looking for talented authors. To submit an idea, please send a brief inquiry to acquisitions@foxchapelpublishing.com.

Printed in Singapore
10 9 8 7 6 5 4 3 2 1

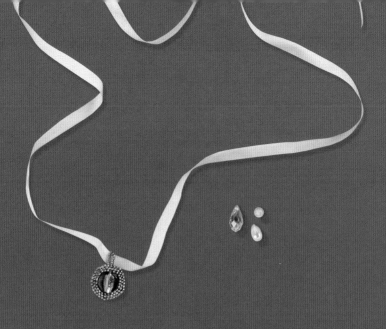

INTRODUCTION

It is great fun to create jewelry and also surprisingly easy. Only basic tools are required, but the most exciting part is the fabulous choice of beads that is widely available. Once you start making jewelry with beautiful semiprecious, glass, and crystal beads, you will not want to use anything else.

The projects in this book cater to all tastes and are accompanied by concise step-by-step instructions to help you achieve a professional standard. There is a variation given for each project to show the versatility of both the design and materials used. Most pieces are quick to make, and once you have tackled a project, you can adapt the technique to make a matching necklace, bracelet, or set of earrings.

Be inspired to use the techniques in this book to create your own designs. Handcrafted jewelry makes wonderful gifts for friends and family—if you can bear to part with your work!

Contents

Memory Wire Ring

Three-Strand Bracelet

Two-Way Necklace

Flower Drop Earrings

Bound Bangle

Rosette Cuff

Ribbon-Tied Necklace

Asymmetrical Necklace

Two-Strand Necklace

Chunky Stone Necklace

Wire Leaf Choker

Starburst Brooch

78

Woven Butterfly Ring

83

Chain and Bead Necklace

88

Chain Drop Earrings

93

Three-Strand Choker

98

Multistrand Bracelet

103

Tied Flower Lariat

107

Ladder Bracelet

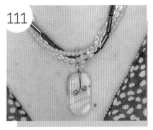
111

Twisted Necklace

116

Rosette Brooch

121

Cluster Stud Earrings

124

Hoop Earrings

127

Spiral Ring

131

Woven Bead Lariat

Equipment

A surprisingly small amount of equipment is needed to make jewelry. For comfort and safety, work on a well-lit, flat, and clean surface. Keep sharp tools and materials beyond the reach of young children. Arrange beads on a nonslip surface so they do not run away when working out designs; a towel or piece of felt is ideal. Work on a white or light-colored surface, as a vividly colored background will affect the appearance of the beads' colors. Alternatively, use a bead board, which has U-shaped grooves in which to arrange beads when designing a necklace.

TOOLS

1. **Tape measure and ruler:** keep a tape measure and ruler handy. For a bracelet, measure the wrist with a tape measure. To measure the length of a necklace, use a length of flexible beading wire, because a tape measure will not drape in the same way.

2. **Wire cutters:** use jewelry wire cutters to cut wire, including flexible beading wire.

3. **Needle-nose pliers:** these versatile pliers have flat-faced jaws to hold work in progress and to close clamshell crimps and cord ends.

4. **Round-nose pliers:** used to make neat loops.

5. **Crimping pliers:** secure crimp beads with crimping pliers for a professional finish to your jewelry.

6. **Plastic-tipped pliers:** the broad plastic jaws of these pliers should be used on delicate projects to prevent damaging the piece you are working on.

7. **Scissors:** cut threads, cord, and ribbon with embroidery scissors. Fine wire can be cut with an old pair of scissors, but the metal will blunt the scissors.

8. **Needles:** thread tiny beads and work bead-weaving projects with beading needles, which come in short and long lengths and are very fine. Collapsible eye needles are flexible twisted wire needles, where the eye squeezes closed to pull through bead holes.

9. **Masking tape:** use this low-tack adhesive tape to wrap around thread, bead cord, and flexible beading wire to keep beads from slipping off and to hold work temporarily in place.

10. **Mandrel:** use a ring mandrel to form wire rings.

11. **Bead loom:** weave a band of small beads on a bead loom to make a lariat, choker, or bracelet.

12. **Bead reamer:** enlarge the holes of glass and stone beads with a diamond-tipped bead reamer. Apply gentle pressure when reaming to avoid chipping the bead.

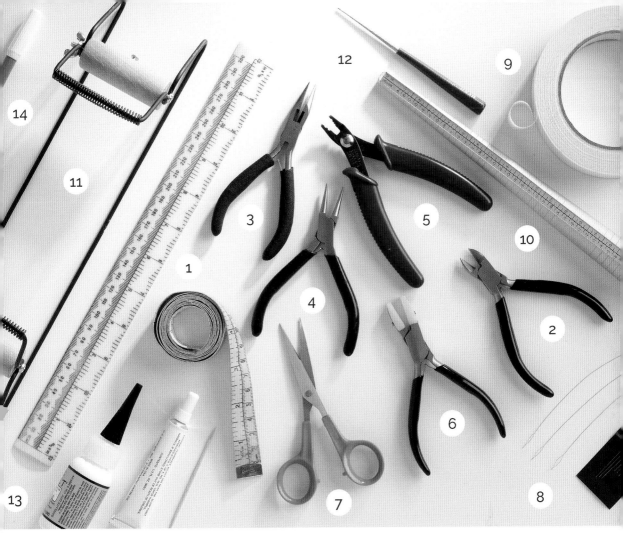

13. **Adhesive:** use cyanoacrylate adhesive or jewelry adhesive (such as E6000) to secure thread knots and to fill the gap between the join of a jump ring or single loop. Apply a tiny dot of adhesive through a fine nozzle or with the tip of a toothpick. Clear nail polish can also be used on jewelry findings, as well as to stiffen the ends of cotton cord and ribbon and to prevent them from fraying.

14. **Water- or air-erasable pen:** although not essential, use a water- or air-erasable pen to mark threads and bead cords. This is useful to note the place to stop beading or to position a particular bead. Marks made with a water-erasable pen will disappear when wetted, and marks made with an air-erasable pen will slowly fade away. The pens are available in sewing stores.

BEADS

The following pages showcase a selection of precious and semiprecious beads used throughout this book. Due to the popularity of beads, many small bead shops have sprung up recently, and they are veritable treasure troves of goodies. The internet gives access to an endless selection of unusual beads and components without having to leave the comfort of your home. Also consider taking apart old, broken jewelry to reuse the beads.

Beads get everywhere! Small beads such as delicas and rocailles are usually supplied in seal-top bags or plastic cylinders with plug-in lids. These containers are good for storing small items as they do not take up much space and are transparent for easy identification. Clear, stubby containers with screw-on lids are widely available in different sizes. These containers are versatile, as the wide opening allows you to slip a needle through the mass of beads to pick one up.

Tip large beads into shallow bowls or saucers while working. Keep beads in sealed containers to protect them from dust, and store all beads away from direct sunlight.

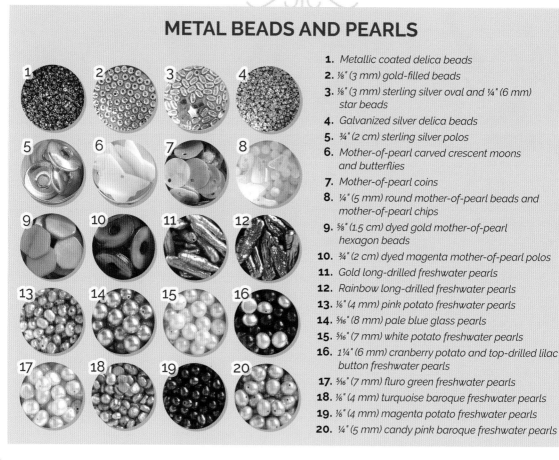

METAL BEADS AND PEARLS

1. Metallic coated delica beads
2. ⅛" (3 mm) gold-filled beads
3. ⅛" (3 mm) sterling silver oval and ¼" (6 mm) star beads
4. Galvanized silver delica beads
5. ¾" (2 cm) sterling silver polos
6. Mother-of-pearl carved crescent moons and butterflies
7. Mother-of-pearl coins
8. ¼" (5 mm) round mother-of-pearl beads and mother-of-pearl chips
9. ⅝" (1.5 cm) dyed gold mother-of-pearl hexagon beads
10. ¾" (2 cm) dyed magenta mother-of-pearl polos
11. Gold long-drilled freshwater pearls
12. Rainbow long-drilled freshwater pearls
13. ⅛" (4 mm) pink potato freshwater pearls
14. ⅝₆" (8 mm) pale blue glass pearls
15. ⁵⁄₁₆" (7 mm) white potato freshwater pearls
16. 1¼" (6 mm) cranberry potato and top-drilled lilac button freshwater pearls
17. ⁵⁄₁₆" (7 mm) fluro green freshwater pearls
18. ⅛" (4 mm) turquoise baroque freshwater pearls
19. ⅛" (4 mm) magenta potato freshwater pearls
20. ¼" (5 mm) candy pink baroque freshwater pearls

Metal Beads and Pearls

Metal beads: use sterling silver, gold-filled, and vermeil beads as spacers between feature beads to prevent the feature beads from overpowering a design. Delica beads are tiny, cylindrical beads used for bead embroidery and weaving. Twenty-four karat gold, sterling silver, and bronze-coated delicas are available. Bali silver beads are decorated with tiny silver balls and fine wires.

Mother-of-pearl: mother-of-pearl is the iridescent nacre coating inside shells that can be carved into all sorts of shapes and dyes well. Mother-of-pearl and pearl jewelry are known as "organic" jewelry because they are created from a living creature or plant.

Pearls: pearls are created in the shells of salt- and freshwater mollusks and have been popular in jewelry making since ancient Greek and Roman times. Cultured pearls are produced by pearl farmers and harvesters using a technique developed in Japan, a country that to this day provides most of the world's supply. Freshwater pearls are created in mussels and come mostly from China. Glass pearls have a lovely, lustrous pearly coating and a crystal glass core that makes them reassuringly weighty.

Pearls come in all sorts of shapes and sizes, and their names are a good indication of their shape. For instance, stick, coin, button, and potato pearls are all available. White and natural shades are usually associated with pearls, but lots of vibrant colors are also available.

Because pearls are delicate, they can easily be scratched, and this is why there is a knot between each pearl in a traditional string of pearls to prevent them from rubbing together. Store pearls separately from other jewelry and keep them away from contact with perfume and cosmetics.

Glass Beads and Crystals

Handcrafted glass beads are made using ancient techniques. They can incorporate metallic foils or crackles and have all sorts of surface decoration. Mass-produced glass beads are pressed or molded into various shapes and sizes and come in many different finishes and colors.

Crystal is glass with more than 30 percent lead content. It is the lead that gives crystal its highly refractive quality, making it sparkle like a diamond.

Swarovski crystals are the best quality. Crystal beads come in a wide color range and in lots of faceted shapes; bicone crystals are particularly versatile. AB stands for Aurora Borealis and is the iridescent rainbow-like coating given to some crystals. AB2X is a variant of AB.

GLASS BEADS AND CRYSTALS

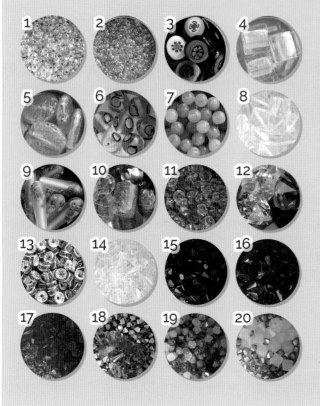

1. *Iridescent glass rocaille beads*
2. *Gold glass rocaille beads*
3. *Millefiori beads*
4. *½" (1.2 cm) pink square foiled glass beads*
5. *¾" (2 cm) gold oval dichroic glass beads*
6. *⅜" (1 cm) lilac lampwork beads*
7. *¼" (5 mm) pink pressed glass beads*
8. *5⁄16" (8 mm) clear faceted square beads*
9. *Blue drop lampwork beads*
10. *Assorted handmade glass beads*
11. *¼" (6 mm) tanzanite spacer crystal beads*
12. *Faceted heart crystal beads*
13. *Metal rondelles studded with crystals*
14. *5⁄16" (8 mm) clear bicone crystal beads*
15. *¼" (6 mm) fuchsia bicone and amethyst crystal beads*
16. *5⁄16" (8 mm) siam bicone crystal beads*
17. *⅛" (4 mm) sapphire bicone crystal beads*
18. *5⁄16" (8 mm) indicolite and ⅛" (4 mm) jet AB bicone crystal beads*
19. *⅛" (4 mm) mixed bicone crystal beads*
20. *⅛" (4 mm) amethyst AB2X and ¼" (6 mm) violet opal bicone crystal beads*

Rocaille beads are small, inexpensive beads that are sold by weight and are used for bead weaving and embroidery. They are available in a huge color range and lots of finishes.

Millefiori means "thousand flowers." These beautiful Venetian beads are created from thin glass rods that are bundled together, then reheated and stretched so that the rods fuse together to make a flower-like pattern.

Lampwork beads are created by using a gas torch to heat glass and wind it around a metal rod to form the base of the bead, which can then be decorated with more molten glass.

Dichroic glass beads have a thin layer of metal fused to the surface, which gives a metallic sheen that changes when viewed from different angles.

Semiprecious Beads

A semiprecious stone is a natural stone mined from the earth that is not classed as a gemstone. Buying semiprecious chips is an inexpensive way of using a favorite stone.

Each month has a birthstone and many wedding anniversaries have designated stones, too. Bear this in mind and incorporate the relevant semiprecious beads if you are making jewelry as a gift. Many stones are even believed to have healing qualities, which could make them a thoughtful feature in a gift. For instance, calcite is said to ease back pain, coral teething troubles, and rose quartz the pain of a broken heart.

The shine of semiprecious stone can be dulled by perfume and natural body oil. Polish semiprecious jewelry with a dry cloth. If necessary, soak the jewelry in lukewarm water with a gentle antibacterial dish soap. Rinse, then pat the jewelry dry.

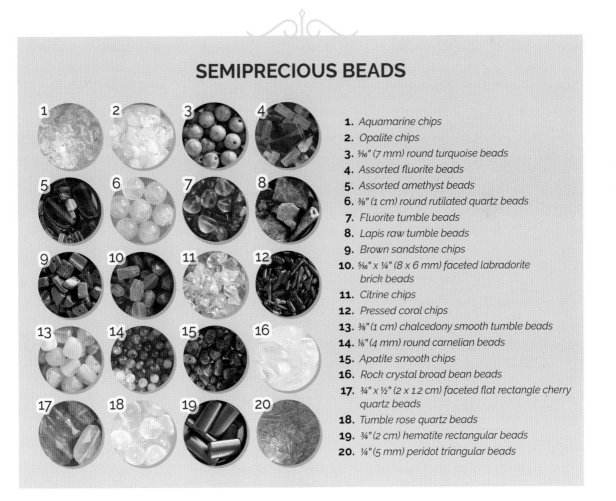

SEMIPRECIOUS BEADS

1. Aquamarine chips
2. Opalite chips
3. ⁵⁄₁₆" (7 mm) round turquoise beads
4. Assorted fluorite beads
5. Assorted amethyst beads
6. ⅜" (1 cm) round rutilated quartz beads
7. Fluorite tumble beads
8. Lapis raw tumble beads
9. Brown sandstone chips
10. ⁵⁄₁₆" x ¼" (8 x 6 mm) faceted labradorite brick beads
11. Citrine chips
12. Pressed coral chips
13. ⅜" (1 cm) chalcedony smooth tumble beads
14. ⅛" (4 mm) round carnelian beads
15. Apatite smooth chips
16. Rock crystal broad bean beads
17. ¾" x ½" (2 x 1.2 cm) faceted flat rectangle cherry quartz beads
18. Tumble rose quartz beads
19. ¾" (2 cm) hematite rectangular beads
20. ¼" (5 mm) peridot triangular beads

Bead Strings and Feature Beads

Most semiprecious beads are available strung rather than loose. Some come on silk cord ready to be made into necklaces or bracelets. Distinctive feature beads are sold individually and are great to use as pendants. Keep the rest of a necklace or bracelet understated to effectively display a feature bead.

BEAD STRINGS AND FEATURE BEADS

1. ¼" (6 mm) square turquoise beads
2. ⅛" (4 mm) square carnelian beads
3. ⁵⁄₁₆" (7 mm) round pink opal beads
4. Agate side-drilled oval bead
5. Fire agate agogo pendant
6. Amethyst side-drilled bead
7. Moonstone pendant
8. Dyed jade carved leaves
9. ¼" (6 mm) flat round pink quartz beads
10. ½" (2 mm) round turquoise beads
11. ⅜" x ⁵⁄₁₆" (1 cm x 8 mm) rectangular blue calcite beads

THREADING MATERIAL

Beads can be strung on a variety of threading materials. The size of the hole in the bead often determines the threading material. Many freshwater pearls have very small holes. This is because they are sold in bulk by weight, and the smaller the hole, the heavier the bead! Therefore, use a fine bead cord or nylon thread with a very fine beading needle. Beads with larger holes can be threaded on cord and ribbon or suspended on ball pins and head pins.

Make bracelets and necklaces any length you wish. Here are standard finished lengths:

Bracelet: 7"–8" (18–20 cm)

Choker: 13"–15" (33–38 cm)

Princess necklace: 18" (45 cm)

Matinee necklace: 24" (60 cm)

1. **Carded bead cord:** this twisted silk bead cord has a stainless steel needle already attached to one end. It comes in different thicknesses and many colors.

2. **Flexible beading wire:** fine wires are twisted together and coated with nylon to make this strong wire. The more strands of wire used, the more flexible the wire is. There are 7-strand, 19-strand, and 49-strand wires available. All come in different thicknesses and a range of colors. The most versatile of the range is the 19-strand wire.

3. **Fine bead cord:** available on a reel, this synthetic twisted cord is extremely strong and will not stretch.

4. **Nylon thread:** strong nylon thread can come in a large choice of colors. Use nylon thread for stringing small beads and bead weaving.

5. **Quilting thread:** although not a usual beading thread, this strong thread is economical to use when a large quantity of thread is needed— for a bead loom project, for example. Run the thread over beeswax to keep it from tangling.

6. **Cord and ribbon:** consider other materials for threading beads. A simple necklace of ribbon or cotton or leather cord will set off a pendant beautifully.

7. **Wire:** use sterling silver or gold-filled wire with semiprecious beads. The thickness of wire is measured in gauges; the higher the number, the thinner the wire.

8. **26 gauge (0.4 mm) wire:** this size wire is useful for making findings and twisting together.

9. **18 gauge (1 mm) half-hard wire:** bend this wire with pliers to make pendants and rings. It can be filed with a jewelry file or a metal manicure file.

10. **Memory wire:** this coiled wire always returns to its original shape. Use memory wire shears or strong wire cutters to cut it. It comes in three sizes that are suitable for making rings, bracelets, and chokers. To finish and prevent beads from slipping off, bend the wire back on itself or glue on a stop bead at each end.

11. **French wire:** also known as bullion or gimp, French wire is a narrow tube of twisted wire. Use it to cover and protect bead cord from rubbing against a clasp.

12. **Chain:** various types of chain are available by the yard (meter) and are often sold in convenient half-yard lengths. Attach beads to a chain with head pins, ball pins, eye pins, or jump rings.

FINDINGS

Findings are the metal components that turn your beaded creations into jewelry. Do justice to your semiprecious beads by using good-quality sterling silver, gold-filled, and vermeil findings. Silver is too soft to be durable alone, so a little of another metal, usually copper, is added to increase its hardness. To be defined as silver, metal must be 92.5 percent silver—which includes sterling silver. Gold-filled findings are a realistic alternative to real gold. Gold-filled means that a solid layer of gold has been bonded to a base metal, which is often brass. Vermeil (or gilded silver) has a sterling silver base coated with gold.

1. **Head pins** and **ball pins:** head pins resemble long dressmaking pins, while ball pins have a small, distinctive ball at the end. Both are available in different lengths. 1⅜" (3.5 cm) and 2" (5 cm) lengths are the most versatile and are used in the projects in this book. A bead or beads are threaded onto the pin and a loop is made above for hanging.

2. **Eye pins:** eye pins have a loop (an "eye") at one end. Use eye pins to pin beads or to attach to the ends of bead strings; the eye is then hidden in an end cap. You can make your own eye pins by turning a loop at the end of a length of wire.

3. **Jump rings:** these small rings join components together. Jump rings come in different sizes and are usually round, but oval jump rings are also available. Join a row of jump rings together to make a chain.

4. **Closed rings:** a closed ring does not open, so anything that is suspended from it needs to open. A closed ring can be a feature of a piece of jewelry.

5. **Crimp beads:** these tiny metal cylinders are squeezed closed to secure the ends of beading wire to a clasp or other component. Attach crimp beads with a pair of crimping pliers.

6. **End bars:** finish a multistrand necklace or bracelet with a pair of end bars to separate the bead strings. These come in various styles with different numbers of holes for affixing the strings of beads. Some clasps incorporate end bars.

7. **Spacer bars:** spacer bars have a row of drilled holes to separate strings of beads. Use spacer bars that coordinate with your end bars.

8. **End caps:** also called bell caps, these caps will conceal the ends of multistrand necklaces or bracelets to create a neat finish.

9. **Clamshell crimps:** finish necklaces or bracelets strung on bead string or thread with clamshell crimps, which have two hinged cups to hide the knotted end of strung beads.

10. **Clasps:** there is a beautiful and versatile range of clasps available to fasten necklaces and bracelets.

11. **Extension chain:** use an extension chain to lengthen a necklace. A bead can be attached to the end of the chain to coordinate with the necklace.

12. **Cord ends:** the ends of thick cord are dabbed with glue and inserted into a cord end, which is then squeezed closed with a pair of needle-nose pliers to hold the cord in place. A hole at the end of the cord end is attached to a clasp.

13. **Earring wires:** hang beaded pieces on ear studs or hooks. Ear clips are also available for unpierced ears. Hoops come in different sizes and are great for making flamboyant, gypsy-style earrings.

14. **Sieves and backs:** sieves are perforated disks that beads can be sewn to with wire or to which beads on head pins or ball pins can be attached. The sieves are then affixed with small prongs to a brooch, ear clip, or ring back.

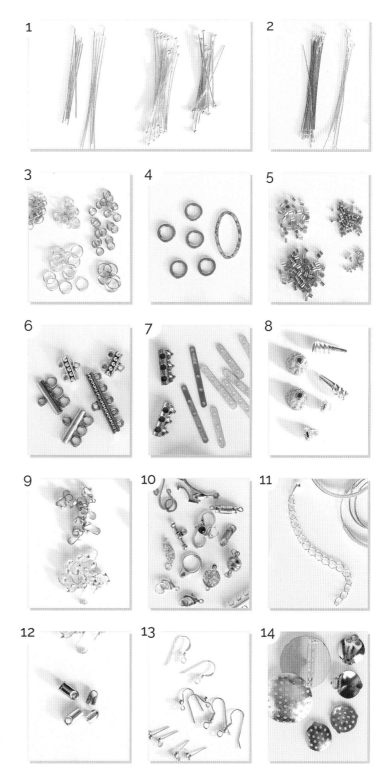

Techniques

The techniques described in this section are used throughout the book. Before embarking on a project, read all the instructions carefully to make sure that you are familiar with the techniques used. Always follow either US or metric measurements, but never a combination of both.

MAKING A SINGLE LOOP

Beads attached to ball pins and head pins can be hung from a chain or a pair of earrings to create jewelry in an instant. The closer you hold the wire to the tip of the jaws of a pair of round-nose pliers, the smaller the loop will be. The further up the jaws you hold the wire, the larger the loop will be. To make beads with single loops of a uniform size, always hold the wire at the same position. A small strip of masking tape wrapped around one jaw can act as a guide for positioning the loop.

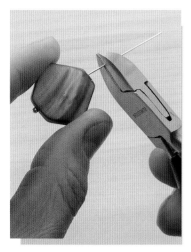
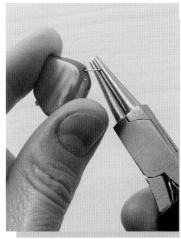

1. Slip a bead or beads onto a ball pin, head pin, or eye pin. Start with a small bead if the other bead holes are large and prone to slip off the ball of a ball pin or the head of a head pin. Cut off the excess wire 5/16" (7 mm) above the last bead with wire cutters. Leave a longer length of wire if you want to make a larger loop.

2. Hold the end of the wire with a pair of round-nose pliers. Bend the wire away from you at a right angle on top of the last bead.

3. Turn your wrist to curl the wire toward you as far as is comfortable to make a loop. Release the wire and grab it again to continue rolling it into a loop. It should resemble a closed circle. If you wish, apply a dab of cyanoacrylate adhesive, jewelry adhesive, or clear nail polish on the join to secure the loop.

MAKING A WRAPPED LOOP

A wrapped loop is closed securely, making it suitable for heavy beads. It is easier to wrap with a fine wire, but use thick wire for very heavy beads.

1. Slip a bead or beads onto a ball pin or head pin. Start with a small bead if the other bead holes are large and prone to slip off the ball of a ball pin or the head of a head pin. Hold the wire with the tips of a pair of needle-nose pliers, resting the jaws on the last bead. Using your fingers, bend the wire over the jaws at a right angle.

2. Hold the wire with a pair of round-nose pliers close to the bend in the wire. Roll the wire over the jaw of the pliers toward you as far as is comfortable to make a loop.

3. Release the wire and grab it again to continue rolling it into a loop, ending up with the wire again at a right angle to the wire coming from the bead.

4. With the round-nose pliers slipped through the loop to hold the wire steady, wrap the extending wire neatly around the wire coming from the bead.

5. Snip off the excess wire close to the bead.

6. Squeeze the snipped end close to the wrapped wire with a pair of needle-nose pliers.

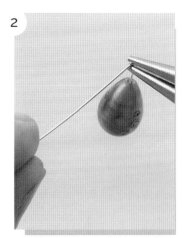

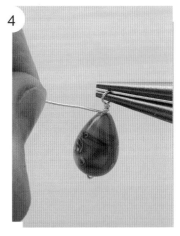

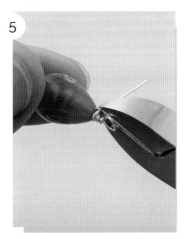

MAKING PINNED BEADS

Pinned beads are beads threaded onto wire or an eye pin with a loop on each side. The loops can be joined together to make a length of pinned beads. If you are using an eye pin, start at Step 3. If you intend to make a number of pinned beads, wrap a small strip of masking tape around one jaw of a pair of round-nose pliers to mark the place to hold the wire when making the loop. This will ensure that the loops are all the same size.

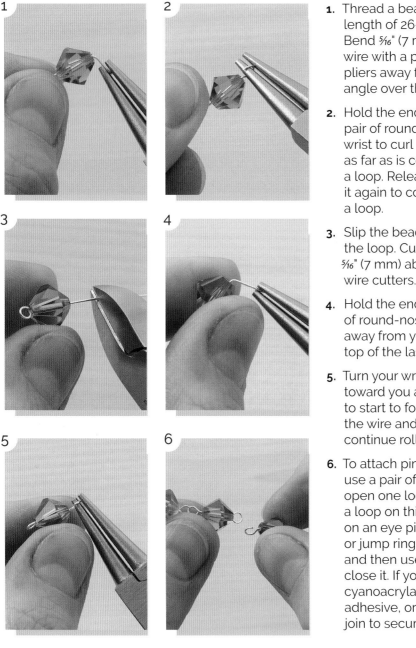

1. Thread a bead or beads onto a length of 26-gauge (0.4 mm) wire. Bend ⁵⁄₁₆" (7 mm) at one end of the wire with a pair of round-nose pliers away from you at a right angle over the pliers.

2. Hold the end of the wire with a pair of round-nose pliers. Turn your wrist to curl the wire toward you as far as is comfortable to make a loop. Release the wire and grab it again to continue rolling it into a loop.

3. Slip the beads down the wire to the loop. Cut off the excess wire ⁵⁄₁₆" (7 mm) above the last bead with wire cutters.

4. Hold the end of the wire with a pair of round-nose pliers. Bend the wire away from you at a right angle on top of the last bead.

5. Turn your wrist to curl the wire toward you as far as is comfortable to start to form the loop. Release the wire and grab it again to continue rolling it into a loop.

6. To attach pinned beads together, use a pair of round-nose pliers to open one loop. If you are opening a loop on thicker wire, such as on an eye pin, slip a closed loop or jump ring onto the open loop and then use two pairs of pliers to close it. If you wish, apply a dab of cyanoacrylate adhesive, jewelry adhesive, or clear nail polish on the join to secure the loop.

MAKING A WRAPPED SIDE- OR TOP-DRILLED BEAD

Use this method to affix a side- or top-drilled bead onto wire. Making a wrapped loop above the bead will secure it in place.

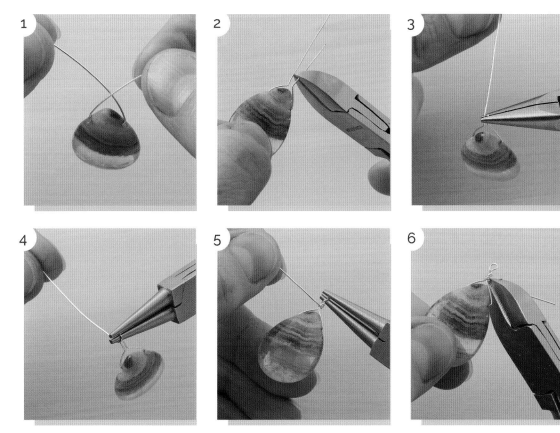

1. Slip a side-drilled bead onto a 3¼" (8 cm) length of 26-gauge (0.4 mm) wire with ¾" (2 cm) of the wire extending on one side. Pull the wires tightly across the top of the bead.

2. Use a pair of needle-nose pliers to bend each wire upwards at the point where the two wires cross. Snip the short end of wire ⅛" (3 mm) above the top of the bead with wire cutters.

3. Hold the wires with a pair of needle-nose pliers, resting the jaws on the bead. Bend the extending wire over the jaws at a right angle.

4. Make a loop above the bend in the wire using a pair of round-nose pliers, ending up with the wire again at a right angle to the wire coming from the bead.

5. With the round-nose pliers slipped through the loop to hold the wire steady, wrap the extending wire neatly around both wires coming from the bead.

6. Snip off the excess wire close to the bead. Squeeze the snipped end close to the wrapped wire with a pair of needle-nose pliers.

USING A CRIMP BEAD

Crimp beads resemble small metal beads. They are easy to secure in place with a pair of crimping pliers. A pair of needle-nose pliers will suffice to flatten the crimp, but will not give the neat, rounded shape that you can achieve with crimping pliers.

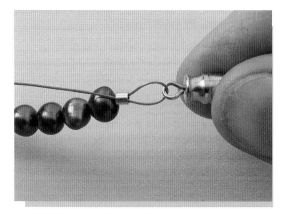

1. Slip a crimp bead onto flexible beading wire, usually after completing the beading for a necklace or bracelet. Thread on a clasp, jump ring, or other jewelry component. Pull the end of the beading wire back through the crimp bead, leaving a small loop of beading wire around the component that is just loose enough to allow for some movement.

2. Place the crimp bead in the inner notch of a pair of crimping pliers. Squeeze the pliers closed. The squashed crimp will be crescent shaped.

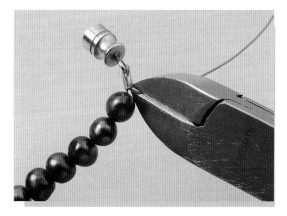

3. Now, place the crimp bead in the outer notch of the pliers. Squeeze the pliers closed. This will round the shape of the crimp. Release and turn the crimp in the notch and close the pliers again to improve the shape.

4. Use wire cutters to snip off the excess beading wire as close as possible to the crimp.

USING JUMP RINGS

Jump rings are used throughout the projects in this book. It is important to open and close jump rings sideways. Do not pull jump rings open outwards, as they will weaken and possibly snap.

1. Hold the jump ring with a pair of pliers on one side of the opening and another pair of pliers on the other side of the opening. For instance, use a pair of needle-nose pliers and a pair of round-nose pliers. Open the jump ring by gently pulling one pair of pliers toward you until the opening is large enough for what you need to slip onto the jump ring.

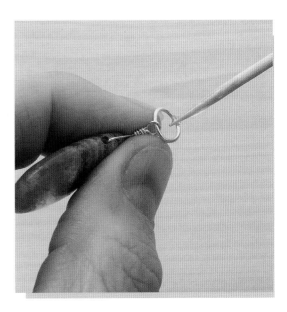

2. Push the same pair of pliers away from you to close the jump ring, making sure the opening is realigned. For extra security, dab the opening with cyanoacrylate adhesive, jewelry adhesive, or clear nail polish. Use the tip of a toothpick to apply a tiny amount of adhesive or nail polish.

PROJECTS

Memory Wire Ring

Memory wire is a stiff, spring-like wire that returns to its tightly coiled form when it is expanded and released. This memory wire ring is threaded with sparkling crystals and dotted with silver stars. Make a few rings in contrasting colors for maximum effect.

You Will Need

- Silver-plated ring memory wire
- Memory wire shears or strong wire cutters
- Round-nose pliers
- 76 x ⅛" (3 mm) indicolite bicone crystal beads
- 3 sterling silver ¼" (6 mm) star beads

2. Pull open the coils and thread on seventeen ⅛" (3 mm) indicolite bicone crystal beads. Slip the crystal beads along the wire to the loop.

1. Separate five coils from the main body of the silver-plated ring memory wire. Cut off coils using memory wire shears or strong wire cutters. Bend one end of the wire into a small loop with the tips of a pair of round-nose pliers. It is important to bend memory wire in the opposite direction of its natural curve.

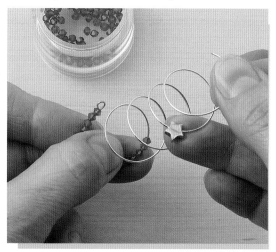

3. Thread on a sterling silver star bead. Thread on twenty-two crystal beads.

TIP:

Memory wire is very strong.
Do not use ordinary jewelry
wire cutters to cut it. Always
use memory wire shears or
strong wire cutters.

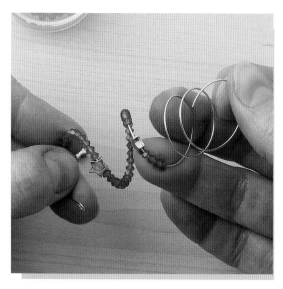

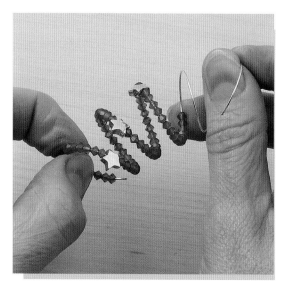

4. Thread on a sterling silver star bead. Thread on twenty-one crystal beads and another star bead.

5. Thread on sixteen crystal beads. Move the crystal beads and stars along the wire to butt up against the loop. Snip the wire ½" (1.2 cm) after the last crystal bead.

6. Bend the end of the wire into a small loop with the tips of a pair of round-nose pliers, remembering to bend the memory wire in the opposite direction of its natural curve.

VARIATION:
This simple memory wire ring is threaded with eighty-two ⅛" (3 mm) bicone crystals in pretty shades of pink and purple.

Three-Strand Bracelet

Semiprecious chips are inexpensive, and their irregular shapes suit the rustic handcrafted look of Bali-style silver beads and findings. This bracelet features an unusual Bali-style bead at the center that anchors three strands of delicately colored aquamarine chips.

You Will Need

- 2 sterling silver eye pins
- 2 sterling silver ⅛" (4 mm) jump rings
- Needle-nose pliers
- Round-nose pliers
- 1 sterling silver toggle clasp set
- 2 sterling silver ⅜" (1 cm) end caps
- 1 string of aquamarine chips
- Wire cutters
- 36" (90 cm) flexible beading wire
- ½" (1.2 cm) Bali-style sterling silver filigree flattened round bead
- Masking tape
- 6 x 1/16" (1 mm) crimp beads
- Crimping pliers

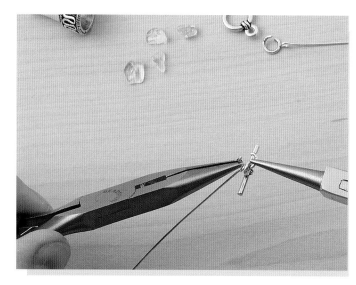

1. To calculate the length of the bracelet, slip the eye of each eye pin onto a ⅛" (4 mm) jump ring. Affix the jump rings onto the ring at each side of a toggle clasp set using two pairs of pliers. Fasten the clasp. Thread two chips and an end cap onto each eye pin.

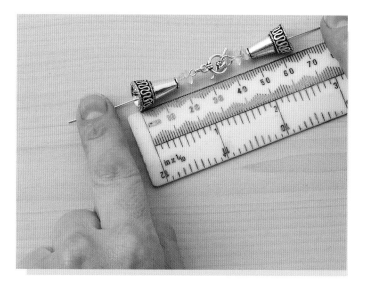

2. Lay the piece flat and measure the length. For the final measurement, subtract this measurement from the desired bracelet length. Use wire cutters to cut three lengths of flexible beading wire 3¼" (8 cm) longer than the final measurement. Remove the eye pins and set the four chips and end caps aside.

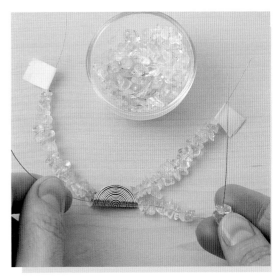

3. Thread a ½" (1.2 cm) Bali-style sterling silver filigree flattened round bead onto the center of one length of flexible beading wire. Thread aquamarine chips onto each end of the beading wire, leaving 1½" (4 cm) at each end. Wrap a piece of masking tape around the ends to keep the chips from sliding off.

4. Slip the second length of beading wire through the silver bead, then thread chips on each end and tape the ends as before. Repeat with the third length of beading wire.

5. Peel the tape off the end of one length of beading wire, then thread on a crimp bead and eye pin. Insert the beading wire back through the crimp bead, leaving a small loop of beading wire through the eye pin that allows for some movement.

6. Refer to the technique on page 22 (Using a Crimp Bead) to secure the crimp bead in place using a pair of crimping pliers. Snip off the excess beading wire with wire cutters. Repeat to secure the other end to an eye pin with a crimp bead.

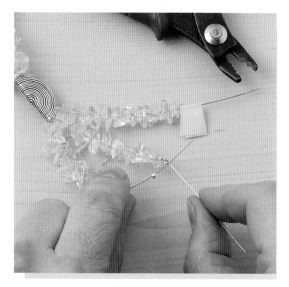

7. Secure the remaining lengths of threaded beading wire to the eye pins in the same way.

8. Thread an end cap onto one eye pin. It will cover the crimped ends of the beading wire. Thread on two aquamarine chips. Refer to the technique on page 19 (Making a Wrapped Loop) to make a wrapped loop above the chips. Repeat on the other end of the bracelet.

9. Use two pairs of pliers to open a jump ring on the clasp. Slip the loop of one wrapped loop onto the jump ring. Close the jump ring using the pliers. Repeat at the other end of the clasp.

VARIATION:

Here is a neat bracelet of three strands of sterling silver beads, red glass rocaille beads, and ⅛" (4 mm) garnet beads.

Two-Way Necklace

This pretty necklace is versatile. It can be slipped over the head and worn as a single long length or worn as a double shorter length that fastens at the front. Choose an attractive toggle clasp, as it will be a feature of the necklace. The hoop part of the clasp suspends some choice beads—add as many as you wish.

You Will Need

- 36" (90 cm) flexible beading wire
- Wire cutters
- 4 gold crimp beads
- 1 x ⅝" (1.5 cm) vermeil toggle clasp set
- Crimping pliers
- 2 x 14" (35 cm) strings of magenta ⅙" (4 mm) baroque freshwater pearls
- 1 x ¾" (1.8 cm) light blue drop lampwork bead
- 4 x 1⅜" (3.5 cm) gold-filled ball pins
- Needle-nose pliers
- Round-nose pliers
- 1 x ⁵⁄₁₆" (8 mm) padparadscha drop crystal
- 1 mother-of-pearl chip
- 1 rose quartz chip
- 2 x ⅙" (4 mm) light azore bicone crystals
- 1 x ¼" (6 mm) light colorado faceted rondelle
- 1 x ⅛" (3 mm) rose alabaster bicone crystal
- 5 x ⁵⁄₃₂" x ¼" (7 x 5 mm) gold-filled oval jump rings
- 1 fuchsia crystal pendant
- Cyanoacrylate adhesive or jewelry adhesive

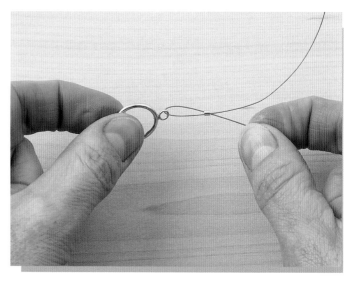

1. Cut an 18" (45 cm) length of flexible beading wire with a pair of wire cutters. Slip a crimp bead and then the hoop of a ⅝" (1.5 cm) vermeil toggle clasp set onto one end. Insert the end of the beading wire through the crimp bead, suspending the hoop.

2. Secure the crimp bead using a pair of crimping pliers, referring to the technique on page 22 (Using a Crimp Bead). Snip off the excess beading wire with wire cutters.

3. Set aside a freshwater pearl from each string of pearls. Thread one string of pearls onto the beading wire.

4. Slip on a crimp bead and the ring of the bar half of the clasp. Insert the end of the beading wire through the crimp bead, suspending the bar.

5. Secure the crimp bead using a pair of crimping pliers as before. Snip off the excess beading wire with wire cutters. Repeat Steps 1 to 5 to affix a second string of pearls between the clasp.

6. Slip a ¾" (1.8 cm) light blue drop lampwork bead and one of the remaining pearls onto a 1⅜" (3.5 cm) gold-filled ball pin. Refer to the technique on page 19 (Making a Wrapped Loop) to secure the bead and pearl in place using two pairs of pliers. Affix a ⁵⁄₁₆" (8 mm) padparadscha drop crystal to a ball pin with a wrapped loop in the same way.

7. Slip a mother-of-pearl chip, a rose quartz chip, the remaining pearl, and a ⅛" (4 mm) light azore bicone crystal onto a ball pin. Slip a ¼" (6 mm) light colorado faceted rondelle, a ⅛" (4 mm) light azore bicone crystal, and a ⅛" (3 mm) rose alabaster bicone crystal onto a ball pin. Secure in place with a wrapped loop.

8. Use the pliers to open five ⁵⁄₃₂" x ¼" (7 x 5 mm) gold-filled oval jump rings. Slip the loop of one of the wrapped loops and the hoop of the clasp onto one jump ring. Close the jump ring securely using both pairs of pliers. Affix the remaining fixed loops and a fuchsia crystal pendant to the hoop in the same way. Carefully apply a little cyanoacrylate adhesive or jewelry adhesive to the join of the jump rings to secure them closed.

VARIATION:

Coral freshwater pearls are used with sterling silver findings on this two-way necklace. The clasp suspends a silver heart charm and glass, pearl, and crystal beads.

Flower Drop Earrings

Delicate flowers carved from glass or semiprecious stones are suspended below mother-of-pearl beads on these pretty earrings. They are simple to make and would be a lovely gift for a bride or bridesmaid. The flowers can hang below as many mother-of-pearl beads as you wish. Here, pink cat's-eye flowers are teamed with nine mother-of-pearl beads.

You Will Need

- 16" (40 cm) flexible beading wire
- Wire cutters
- 2 x ⅝" (1.5 cm) pink cat's-eye (glass) carved flowers with center hole
- 18 x ⅛" (4 mm) mother-of-pearl beads
- 2 gold-filled crimp beads
- 2 gold-filled hook earring wires
- Crimping pliers

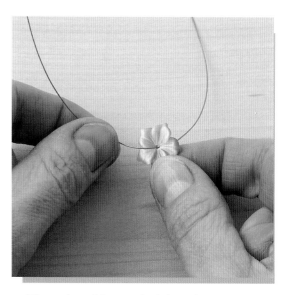

1. Thread a ⅝" (1.5 cm) pink cat's-eye (glass) carved flower with a center hole onto an 8" (20 cm) length of flexible beading wire. Slip the flower along the beading wire to the center.

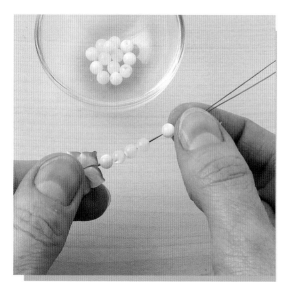

2. Bring the ends of the beading wire together and thread on nine ⅛" (4 mm) mother-of-pearl beads. Thread on fewer beads if you prefer a shorter drop.

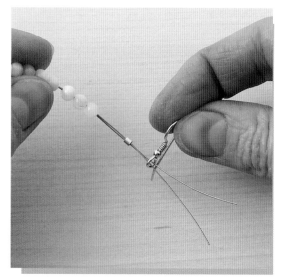

3. Insert the ends of the beading wire through a crimp bead and the eye of a hook earring wire.

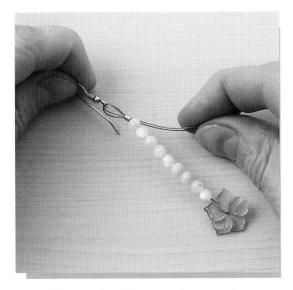

4. Pull the ends of the beading wire to tighten the loop around the earring wire but allow some room for movement. Adjust the flower to face forward as you tighten the beading wire.

5. Secure the crimp bead using a pair of crimping pliers, referring to the technique on page 22 (Using a Crimp Bead).

6. Snip off the excess beading wire close to the crimp bead with wire cutters. Make a matching earring.

VARIATION:
Dazzling violet crystal flowers hang below ten ⅛" (3 mm) bicone crystals on these glamorous earrings.

Bound Bangle

This twinkling, chunky bangle studded with sequins and crystals started life as a humble wooden bangle. The bangle is bound with pale gold rocaille beads with sequins and crystals applied at random.

You Will Need

- Short beading needle
- Quilting thread
- Wooden or plastic bangle
- Cyanoacrylate adhesive
- 40 g (1½ oz) of size 11 pale gold glass rocaille beads
- Masking tape
- Approx. 48 gold cup sequins
- Approx. 48 x ⅛" (4 mm) bicone crystal beads in shades of green, turquoise, and brown

1. Thread a short beading needle with a 60" (150 cm) double length of quilting thread. Knot the ends together. Slip the needle through the middle of the bangle and insert the needle between the threads. Pull the threads tight and glue the knot to the inside of the bangle.

2. Thread on about fifty rocaille beads. Slip the beads down the thread to the knot. Wrap the bead-strung thread around the bangle. Stick a piece of masking tape inside the bangle to hold the strung beads in place.

TIP:
Use a bangle similar in color to the rocaille beads. Remember that the bangle will be a tighter fit once it has been beaded.

3. Continue threading on beads. Wrap the beaded thread tightly around the bangle until there are one and a half rows of beads on the outside of the bangle. Insert the needle up through a cup sequin, then thread on a bicone crystal bead.

4. Insert the needle back through the sequin. Pull the thread so that the sequin rests on the last rocaille bead with the crystal bead on the center of the sequin.

5. Now insert the needle through the last rocaille bead, toward the free end of thread.

6. Continue threading on beads and wrapping them closely around the bangle, applying a sequin and crystal bead on the outside of the bangle on alternate rows of beads. Push the rows together so that they cover the bangle. Use masking tape inside the bangle to keep the strung beads together.

7. When the beads are about 6" (15 cm) from the end of the thread, cut off the needle. Bind the thread twice around the bangle and glue in place. Cut off the excess thread.

8. Thread the needle with a 60" (150 cm) double length of quilting thread and knot the ends together. Slip the needle through the middle of the bangle and insert the needle between the threads as before. Pull the threads tight and glue the knot to the inside of the bangle close to the beading. Insert the needle through the last six beads.

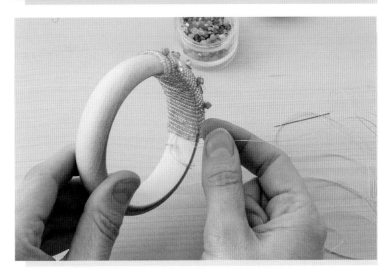

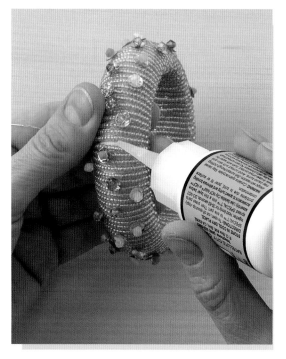

9. Continue beading the bangle, finishing and adding more thread when necessary as described in Steps 7 and 8.

10. Insert the needle through the first six beads. Part the beads and bind the thread a few times around the bangle. Carefully glue the threads to the bangle. Cut off the excess thread.

VARIATION:
This technique is also effective without the sequins and crystals, as shown on this narrow bangle bound with shiny red glass rocaille beads.

Rosette Cuff

This unusual cuff is made up of sparkling beaded rosettes. The glass bead at the center of each rosette is circled with delicately woven delica beads. The rosettes are joined together and fastened with a beaded loop and glass bead "button."

TIP:
Measure your wrist, allowing room for movement. Subtract ¾" (1.8 cm) from the measurement to allow for the button and loop fastening. Make the strip of rosettes in Step 8 the length of the resulting measurement.

You Will Need

- Nylon thread
- Short beading needle
- Approx. 19 ×
  ½" (1.2 cm) green foil-lined
  disk glass beads
- 20 g (¾ oz) of green
  delica beads

1. Thread a 29½" (75 cm) length of nylon thread onto a short beading needle. Thread the needle through a green foil-lined disk glass bead, leaving an 8" (20 cm) trailing length of thread. Insert the needle through the disk bead again, then repeat, adjusting the threads so that they are on opposite sides of the rim of the bead.

2. Thread on two delica beads. Slip the beads down the thread to rest on the disk bead.

3. Holding the trailing end of thread so that the threads are taut, insert the needle under the first thread.

4. Now insert the needle back up through the last delica bead. Pull the thread so that the delica bead rests on the disk bead. Thread on one delica bead. Repeat Steps 3 and 4 until you have covered the first half of the disk bead.

5. Continue in the same way around the second half of the disk bead. Insert the needle down through the first delica bead, then up through the last delica bead to complete the first ring of beads.

6. Thread on two delica beads to start the second ring of beads. Insert the needle under the thread that is on top of the first ring of beads. Insert the needle up through the second delica bead.

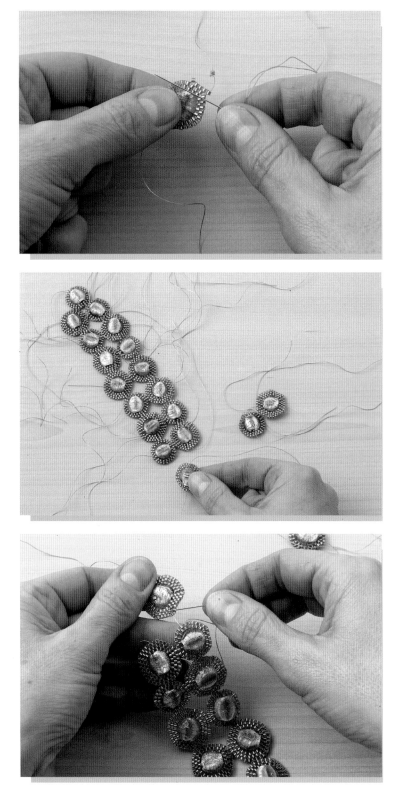

7. Thread on one delica bead. Repeat Step 5 to apply the second ring of beads. Insert the needle down through the first delica bead of the second ring of beads, then up through the last delica bead to complete the second ring of beads. Apply the third ring of delica beads in the same way as the second ring of beads.

8. Make nine rosettes of three rings of beads and nine rosettes of two rings of beads. Leave the ends of threads trailing. To form the cuff, arrange the rosettes touching edge to edge, two deep in a row with a rosette of two rings at each end.

9. Starting at one end of the cuff, join the rosettes together using the trailing ends of threads by weaving the threads between two beads that are side by side on the outer rings where the rosettes butt together. Work the threads through the beadwork and cut off the excess, leaving a thread trailing from the rosette at each end of the cuff.

10. To make a disk glass bead "button," thread a disk bead, then four delica beads onto the thread at one end of the cuff. Slip the beads down the thread. Insert the needle back through the first delica bead and the disk bead.

11. Insert the needle through the next delica bead on the outer ring. Insert the needle through the delica bead where it first emerged to make the button. Repeat Steps 10 and 11 to secure the button, then weave the thread through the beadwork and cut off the excess.

12. Thread enough delica beads onto the thread at the other end of the cuff to loop around the button. Insert the needle through the next bead on the outer ring to make the loop. Insert the needle through the delica bead where it first emerged. Repeat to secure the loop, then weave the thread through the beadwork and cut off the excess.

VARIATION:

A purple foil-lined glass bead has been circled with woven rings of metallic delica beads. The loop at the top means that it can be suspended as a pendant from a length of fine organza ribbon.

Ribbon-Tied Necklace

An eclectic mixture of components and textures are combined to create this fabulous necklace in shades of green. The deep green mother-of-pearl polos have a side-drilled hole that makes them very versatile to use. Bias-cut ribbon is an unusual addition to the necklace.

You Will Need

- 48" (120 cm) flexible beading wire
- Wire cutters
- 17 gold-filled crimp beads
- 7 x ¾" (2 cm) dyed deep green side-drilled mother-of-pearl polos
- Crimping pliers
- 15 x ¼" (6 mm) olive jade rondelle beads
- 11 x ¾" (1.8 cm) lime/turquoise glass coin beads
- 2 olive jade carved leaves
- 31" (80 cm) of ⅝" (1.5 cm)-wide bias ribbon
- Sewing scissors
- 2 x ⁵⁄₁₆" (8 mm) vermeil closed rings
- 2 x ⁵⁄₃₂" x ¼" (7 x 5 mm) gold-filled oval jump rings
- Needle-nose pliers
- Round-nose pliers
- 1 vermeil clasp

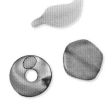

1. Cut a 20" (50 cm) length of flexible beading wire with a pair of wire cutters. Thread a crimp bead onto one end. Insert one end of the beading wire through the center of a polo. Thread the end of the beading wire back through the crimp bead, suspending the polo.

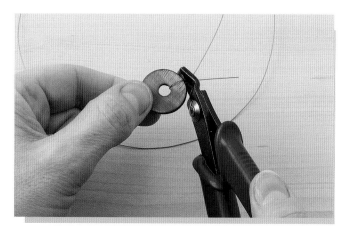

2. Slip the crimp bead along the beading wire to rest against the polo. Secure the crimp bead using a pair of crimping pliers, referring to the technique on page 22 (Using a Crimp Bead). Snip off the excess beading wire with wire cutters.

TIP:
You may need seven large crimp beads to accommodate the two thicknesses of flexible beading wire, and ten small crimp beads to finish the single extending ends of beading wire, as the large size may slip off the single beading wire.

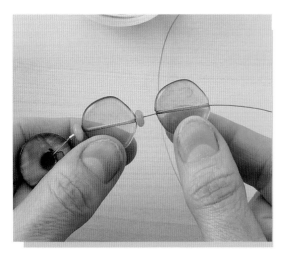

3. Thread on a ¼" (6 mm) olive jade rondelle bead and a ¾" (1.8 cm) lime/turquoise glass coin bead. Repeat twice. Thread on a rondelle bead.

4. Insert the beading wire through a polo, two rondelle beads, two polos, one rondelle, one coin bead, one rondelle, one coin, one carved leaf, one coin, one carved leaf, one polo, one rondelle, one coin, one rondelle, one coin, one rondelle, and one polo. Repeat Step 3.

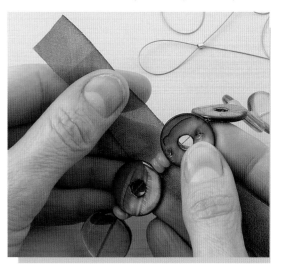

5. Thread on a crimp bead. Insert the beading wire through the center of a polo. Thread the end of the beading wire back through the crimp bead, suspending the polo. Slip the crimp bead along the beading wire to rest between the rondelle and the polo. Secure the crimp bead using a pair of crimping pliers, referring to the technique on page 22 (Using a Crimp Bead). Snip off the excess beading wire with wire cutters.

6. Cut five 4" (12.5 cm) lengths of beading wire with wire cutters. Bend the beading wire in half and insert the ends through a crimp bead. Cut a 5½" (14 cm) length of ribbon with a pair of scissors. Fold the ribbon around the pair of rondelle beads.

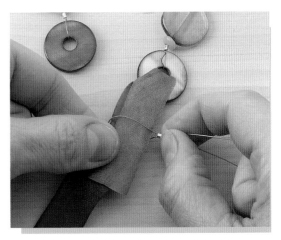

7. Slip one of the beading wire loops over the ends of the ribbon. Slip the crimp bead along the beading wire to tighten the loop around the ribbon. Secure the crimp bead in place with a pair of crimping pliers. Trim the ends of the ribbon with a pair of sewing scissors.

8. Cut two 12" (30 cm) lengths of ribbon. Slip the end of one ribbon through one beading wire loop. Thread 2" (5 cm) at the end of the ribbon through the center of a polo, then through the beading wire loop.

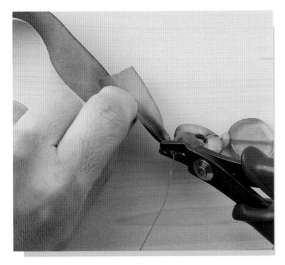

9. Slip the crimp bead along the flexible beading wire and tighten the loop around the ribbon close to the polo. Secure the crimp bead in place with a pair of crimping pliers. Trim the short end of the ribbon with a pair of sewing scissors. Repeat on the polo at the other end of the necklace.

10. Slip the raw end of one ribbon through one beading wire loop. Thread 2" (5 cm) of ribbon through the center of a ⁵⁄₁₆" (8 mm) vermeil closed ring, then through the beading wire loop. Slip the crimp bead along the beading wire to loop it tightly around the ribbon close to the closed ring. Secure the crimp bead in place with a pair of crimping pliers. Trim the short end of the ribbon with a pair of sewing scissors. Repeat on the other ribbon.

 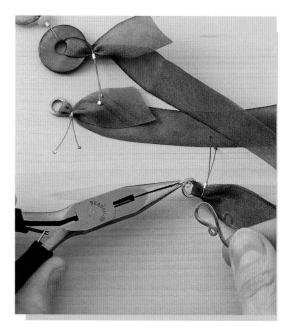

11. Slip a crimp bead onto each extending end of beading wire. Secure the crimp ¾" (2 cm) from the first crimped beads with crimping pliers. Snip off the end of the beading wire with wire cutters close to the crimped beads.

12. Open a ⁵⁄₃₂" x ¼" (7 x 5 mm) gold-filled oval jump ring with two pairs of pliers. Slip the jump ring onto the closed ring and the vermeil clasp. Close the jump ring using the pliers. Repeat at the other end of the necklace.

VARIATION:

Shades of pink have been used on this stunning necklace. Rose quartz rondelle beads are interspersed between dyed magenta mother-of-pearl polos and square foil-lined glass beads. Note that a rondelle bead on each side of the carved leaves allows them to drape comfortably against the square beads.

Asymmetrical Necklace

Each side of this lovely necklace has a different, distinctive look. The necklace fastens at the front by slipping cords knotted with a selection of pretty beads through a loop of freshwater pearls.

TIP:

The double-threaded bead cord may be too thick to insert through some beads. In this case, thread the cords through separately. Alternatively, use a bead reamer to enlarge the holes.

You Will Need

- 2 sterling silver crimp beads
- 18" (45 cm) flexible beading wire
- 34 x ⅛" (4 mm) silver baroque freshwater pearls
- Wire cutters
- Crimping pliers
- 31 x ⁵⁄₁₆" (8 mm) dyed lilac jade beads
- Silver French wire
- No. 10 lilac carded bead cord
- 1 collapsible needle
- 3 x ⅜" (1 cm) lilac donut ceramic beads
- 3 x ⅜" (1 cm) lilac "eye" glass lampwork beads
- 1 x ½" x ⅜" (1.3 cm x 9 mm) lilac drop Bohemian rose lampwork bead
- 3 x 2" (5 cm) sterling silver ball pins
- Needle-nose pliers
- Round-nose pliers
- 4 x ⅛" (3 mm) sterling silver beads
- 2 x 1½" (4 cm)-long lilac handmade glass beads
- Scissors

1. Thread a crimp bead, then sixteen ⅛" (4 mm) silver baroque freshwater pearls onto flexible beading wire. Insert 1½" (4 cm) of one end of the beading wire through the crimp bead, making a loop of threaded pearls.

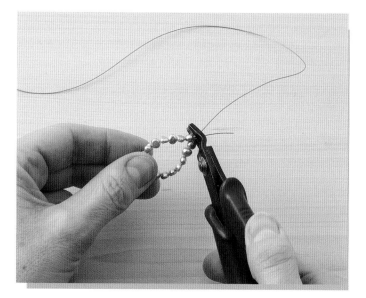

2. Secure the crimp bead using a pair of crimping pliers, referring to the technique on page 22 (Using a Crimp Bead). Snip off the excess beading wire with wire cutters.

3. Thread twenty-eight ⁵⁄₁₆" (8 mm) dyed lilac jade beads onto the beading wire. Slip on a crimp bead, then sixteen ⅛" (4 mm) silver baroque freshwater pearls.

4. Insert the end of the beading wire through the crimp bead, making a loop of threaded pearls. Secure the crimp bead using a pair of crimping pliers as before. Snip off the excess beading wire with wire cutters.

5. Cut a ¾" (2 cm) length of silver French wire with wire cutters. Slip the wire onto the bead cord. Cut the cord to 51" (130 cm) long. Slip the cord through one loop of pearls. Bend the cord in half, then slip the wire along the cord to the center. Thread both ends of cord onto a collapsible needle.

6. Thread on two ⅜" (1 cm) lilac donut ceramic beads. Make a knot after the last bead. Make another knot 1⅜" (3.5 cm) along the cords. Thread on a dyed lilac jade bead. Make a knot after the bead.

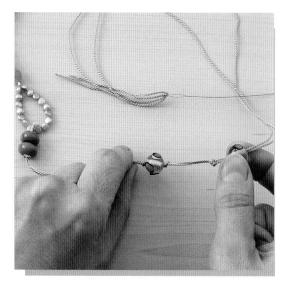

7. Make a knot 1⅜" (3.5 cm) along the cords. Thread on a ⅜" (1 cm) lilac "eye" glass lampwork bead. Make a double knot after the bead. Repeat this step.

9. Slip the wrapped loops of the beads onto the cords. Make a double knot 1⅜" (3.5 cm) from the last knot. Thread a dyed lilac jade bead onto the cords. Make a double knot after the bead. Make a double knot 1⅜" (3.5 cm) from the last knot. Thread a lilac "eye" glass lampwork bead onto both cords. Make a double knot after the bead.

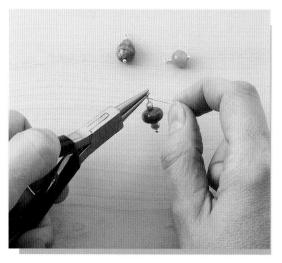

8. Refer to the technique on page 19 (Making a Wrapped Loop) to affix a dyed lilac jade bead onto a ball pin using two pairs of pliers. Affix a ½" x ⅜" (1.3 cm x 9 mm) lilac drop Bohemian rose lampwork bead onto a ball pin with a wrapped loop and a silver baroque freshwater pearl, a lilac donut bead, and another silver baroque freshwater pearl onto another ball pin with a wrapped loop.

10. Pull one cord out of the needle to separate the cords. Make a knot on one cord 1⅜" (3.5 cm) after the last knot and 2¼" (5.5 cm) after the last knot on the other cord.

11. On one cord, thread on a ⅛" (3 mm) sterling silver bead, a 1½" (4 cm)-long lilac handmade glass bead, and another silver bead. Tie the cord tightly around the cord between the long bead and last silver bead.

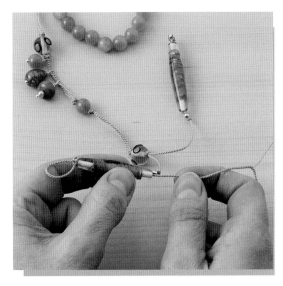

12. Insert the needle back through the long bead. Pull the thread and cut off the excess close to the top of the long bead with a pair of scissors. Repeat Steps 11 and 12 to finish the other cord.

VARIATION:

Here is an asymmetrical choker of mother-of-pearl beads, pale green pearls, and pretty lampwork beads on white bead cord with knots placed 1" (2.5 cm) apart.

Two-Strand Necklace

A variety of beads in delicate shades of smoky gray combine to create this stunning necklace. The strings of fine beads are threaded through a beautiful tube bead of carved jade.

You Will Need

- Wire cutters
- 78" (2 m) flexible beading wire
- Masking tape
- 2 strings of ⅛" (4 mm) silver baroque freshwater pearls
- 1 string of labradorite chips
- Approx. 46 x ⅛" (4 mm) jade disk beads
- 1 string of labradorite faceted brick beads
- 6 x ⅜" (1 cm) rutilated quartz beads
- 1 jade carved tube bead
- 5 sterling silver crimp beads
- Sterling silver clasp
- Crimping pliers

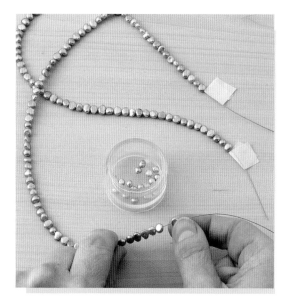

1. Cut two 24" (60 cm) lengths of flexible beading wire with a pair of wire cutters. Tape 1½" (4 cm) at one end of each beading wire with a piece of masking tape to keep the pearls from slipping off. Thread pearls onto the beading wire for 12¼" (31 cm). Tape the end of the beading wire with a piece of masking tape to keep the pearls from slipping off. Repeat on the other beading wire.

2. Cut two 16" (40 cm) lengths of beading wire with a pair of wire cutters. Tape 1½" (4 cm) at one end of each beading wire with a piece of masking tape to keep the beads from slipping off. Thread a sequence of labradorite chips for 1¼" (3 cm), two ⅛" (4 mm) jade disk beads, one labradorite faceted brick bead, and two jade disk beads onto one length of beading wire.

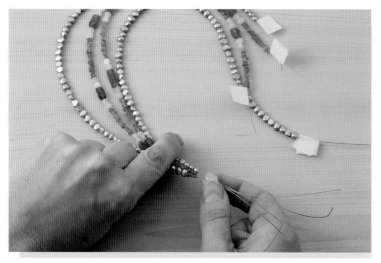

3. Repeat the sequence, adding more labradorite chips to match the threaded length of beads to the threaded lengths of pearls. Repeat on the other beading wire. Remove the end tapes on the pearls. Thread the four threaded beading wires through a ⅜" (1 cm) rutilated quartz bead.

4. Insert the beading wires through a crimp bead. Pull the beading wires tightly through the rutilated quartz bead and crimp. Secure the crimp bead using a pair of crimping pliers, referring to the technique on page 22 (Using a Crimp Bead).

5. Carefully snip off the two shorter beading wires with a pair of wire cutters below the crimp bead. Thread the two beading wires through a jade carved tube bead and a rutilated quartz bead.

6. Thread twelve pearls, one rutilated quartz bead, one crimp bead, and one jade disk bead onto one beading wire. Insert the end of the beading wire back through the crimp bead.

7. Pull the beading wire tightly. Secure the crimp bead using a pair of crimping pliers, referring to the technique on page 22 (Using a Crimp Bead). Snip off the excess beading wire with wire cutters.

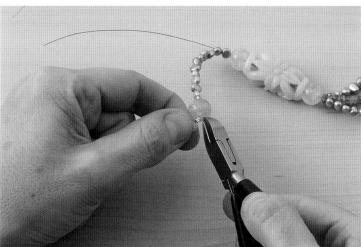

8. Thread labradorite chips for 1" (2.5 cm), two ⅛" (4 mm) jade disk beads, one labradorite faceted brick bead, two jade disk beads, labradorite chips for 1" (2.5 cm), one rutilated quartz bead, one crimp bead, and one jade disk bead onto the other beading wire.

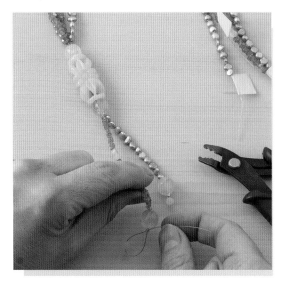

9. Insert the end of the beading wire back through the crimp bead. Repeat Step 7 to secure the crimp bead in place.

10. Remove the masking tape at the start of the beading wires. Insert the beading wire of one string of pearls and beads through a crimp bead and the ring of a sterling silver clasp. Insert the ends of the beading wire back through the crimp bead, suspending the clasp.

VARIATION: *This dramatic necklace has single strands of beads threaded through a pair of round jet beads with a handmade striped glass bead between them. The strands are beaded in a sequence of square jet beads and jet bicone crystal beads.*

11. Secure the crimp bead using a pair of crimping pliers, referring to the technique on page 22 (Using a Crimp Bead). Snip off the excess beading wire with wire cutters. Repeat on the other half of the clasp.

Chunky Stone Necklace

Bold beads strung on silk cord are often knotted to prevent them from rubbing against each other. A knotted cord is used on this stunning necklace of rose quartz and rock crystal beads. A pair of brushed silver beads separates the three distinct sections of the necklace. The necklace is finished with French wire, which will keep the clasp from rubbing against the cord.

TIP:
French wire must be handled gently. Ideally, use the largest size wire you can, as it will uncoil if you try to thread a cord and needle through wire that is too narrow.

You Will Need

- 2½ yd (2 m) of no. 5 pink carded bead cord
- Collapsible needle
- Approx. 24 graduated ⅜"–⅝" (1–1.5 cm) bati rose quartz beads
- Large needle or awl
- 2 brushed sterling silver teardrop beads
- Approx. 9 tumble rose quartz beads
- Approx. 9 rock crystal broad bean beads
- Silver French wire
- Wire cutters
- 1 round sterling silver ball clasp
- Scissors

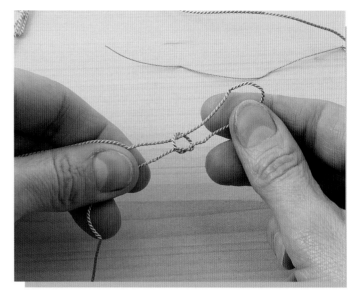

1. If the bead cord does not have an attached needle, thread a 2¼ yd (2 m) length of pink bead cord onto a collapsible needle. Make a loose slipknot about 8" (20 cm) from the end of the cord to keep the beads from slipping off.

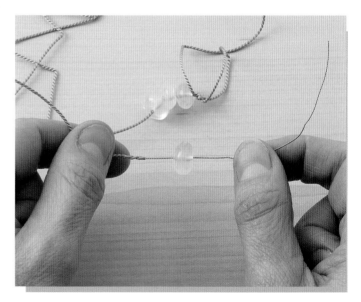

2. Starting with the smallest, thread on the four smallest bati rose quartz beads in order of size. Slip the beads along the cord to the slipknot. The knots for the first four beads will be added later.

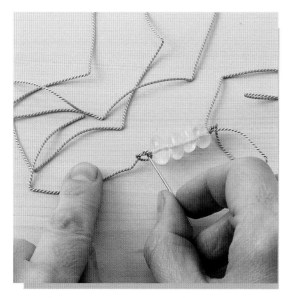

3. Make an overhand knot after the last bead, insert the point of a large needle into the loop of the knot, and guide the knot along the cord to sit next to the bead. Pull the cord to tighten the knot. Make a double knot between all the beads if you prefer a distinctive knot.

4. Thread on the next bead and make a knot as before. The knots should be tight against the beads, as the cord will stretch. Continue adding bati rose quartz beads, graduating the sizes and knotting the cord between the beads.

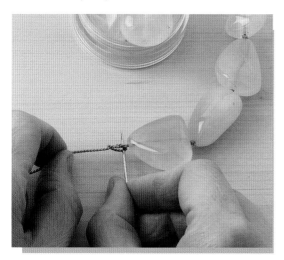

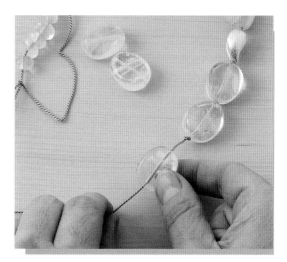

5. Make a knot after the last bead. Thread on a brushed sterling silver teardrop bead. Make a knot. Thread on nine tumble rose quartz beads, knotting the cord between the beads.

6. Make a knot after the last bead. Thread on a brushed sterling silver teardrop bead, facing the opposite direction of the first teardrop bead. Make a knot. Thread on five rock crystal broad bean beads, knotting the cord between the beads.

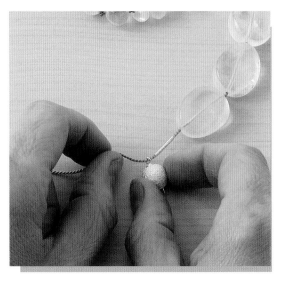

7. Make a knot after the last bead. Thread on four rock crystal broad bean beads.

8. Cut a ⅜" (1 cm) length of silver French wire with wire cutters. Slip the wire along the cord to the last bead. Insert the needle through the ring of the clasp.

9. Insert the needle back through the last bead. Pull up the cord until there is only a small space between the last two beads.

10. Knot the cord tightly around the threaded cord between the last two beads. Insert the needle through the second from last bead. Knot the cord tightly around the threaded cord between the second and third from last two beads.

11. Insert the needle through the third from last bead, then knot the cord tightly around the threaded cord between the third and fourth from last two beads. Insert the needle through the fourth from last bead. Pull the cord taut and cut off the excess with a pair of scissors. The end of the cord will be neatly concealed in the fourth bead.

12. Remove the slipknot at the start of the necklace. Thread the cord onto a collapsible needle. Repeat Steps 8 to 11 to finish the other end of the necklace.

VARIATION: *Here is a bold necklace of raw tumbled lapis beads strung on dark blue carded bead cord. Shiny rock crystal chips at each end of the necklace provide a stark contrast to the lapis beads.*

Wire Leaf Choker

This understated choker displays a pretty leaf pendant to great effect. The pendant is simple to make from half-hard sterling silver wire. Tiny turquoise beads add a contrasting touch of color to the vibrant pink cord.

You Will Need

- 4½" (11.5 cm) of 18-gauge (1 mm) half-hard sterling silver wire
- Jewelry file
- Needle-nose pliers
- Round-nose pliers
- 9 x ½" (2 mm) turquoise beads
- 1 sterling silver eye pin
- Wire cutters
- 20" (50 cm) fine pink cotton cord
- 8 x ⁵⁄₁₆" (8 mm) sterling silver teardrop beads
- 8 x 2" (5 cm) sterling silver ball pins
- Cyanoacrylate adhesive
- 2 sterling silver cord ends
- 1 sterling silver bicone clasp

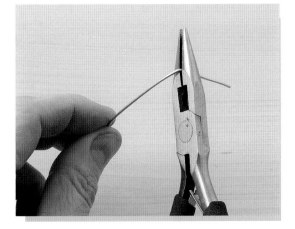

1. File the ends of the wire with a jewelry file to round the ends. Bend 1" (2.5 cm) at one end at right angles to form the "vein" of the leaf using a pair of needle-nose pliers.

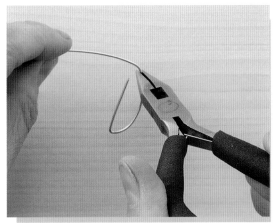

2. Bend the long end of the wire downwards in a curve between your fingers to form the side of the leaf. Bend the wire at a right angle ¼" (6 mm) from the end of the vein using a pair of needle-nose pliers.

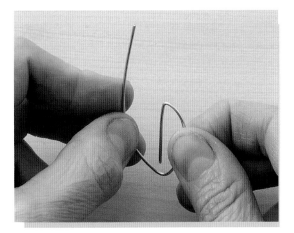

3. Bend the extending wire in a curve between your fingers toward the top of the leaf to form the opposite side of the leaf.

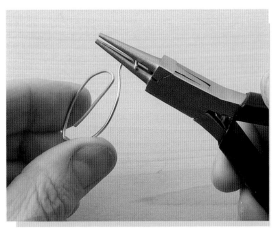

4. Hold the end of the wire with a pair of round-nose pliers. Coil the wire away from the leaf to form a loop.

5. Slip a ½" (2 mm) turquoise bead onto an eye pin. Refer to the technique on page 20 (Making Pinned Beads) to make a pinned bead. Open one eye and slip it onto the loop of the leaf.

6. Insert the fine pink cotton cord through the top eye of the pinned bead. Tie the pinned bead to the center of the cord, suspending the leaf.

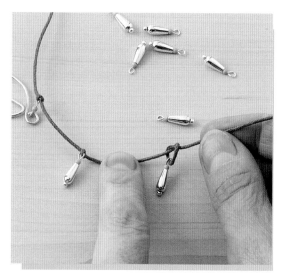

7. Slip a ⁵⁄₁₆" (8 mm) sterling silver teardrop bead and a ½" (2 mm) turquoise bead onto a 2" (5 cm) sterling silver ball pin. Refer to the technique on page 18 (Making a Single Loop) to secure the beads using two pairs of pliers. Repeat to secure beads on eight ball pins.

8. Slip the loop of one ball pin onto the cord. Tie the loop to the cord 1" (2.5 cm) from the center. Repeat to tie three ball pins onto the same side of the cord, tying them in place at 1⅜" (3.5 cm) intervals.

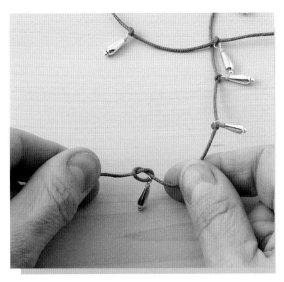

9. Tie the loop of four ball pins in matching positions on the other side of the cord. With the leaf pendant centered, cut the cord 14" (36 cm) long.

10. Dab one end of the cord with cyanoacrylate adhesive and insert it into a cord end. Squeeze the cord end closed around the cord with a pair of needle-nose pliers. Repeat at the other end of the cord.

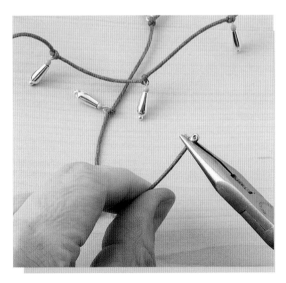

11. Open the loop on a sterling silver bicone clasp using two pairs of pliers. Slip the loop through the eye of one cord end. Close the loop with the pliers. Repeat at the other end of the choker.

VARIATION: *The wire leaves on this delightful pair of earrings are modeled from 3" (7.5 cm) lengths of wire. The leaf "veins" are ⅝" (1.5 cm) long. Each leaf hangs below a pinned candy pink baroque freshwater pearl and a pinned ⅛" (4 mm) light sapphire bicone crystal bead.*

Starburst Brooch

Here is a pretty brooch of assorted semiprecious stone, crystal, and pearl beads. The beads are affixed to twisted wires around a metal sieve that is covered with a mass of beads in lovely shades of sapphire and lilac. A brooch back is attached behind the sieve.

You Will Need

- 3⅓ yd (3 m) of 26-gauge (0.4 mm) sterling silver wire
- Wire cutters
- 1 x 1¼" (3 cm) silver-colored brooch back and sieve
- Needle-nose pliers

- Approx. 13 x ¼" (6 mm) tanzanite spacer crystal beads
- Approx. 12 x ¼" (5 mm) violet faceted crystal beads
- Approx. 12 blue lace agate chips
- Approx. 9 x ¼" (5 mm) violet opal bicone crystal beads

- Approx. 14 x ¼" x ⅛" (6 x 4 mm) rectangular amethyst beads
- Approx. 9 x ⅛" (4 mm) magenta potato freshwater pearl beads
- Approx. 9 x ⅛" (4 mm) mauve potato freshwater pearl beads
- 3 x ⁵⁄₁₆" (8 mm) baby blue side-drilled freshwater pearl beads

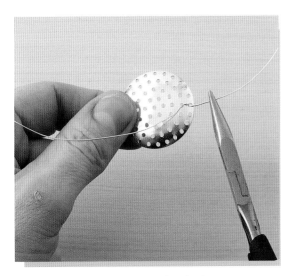

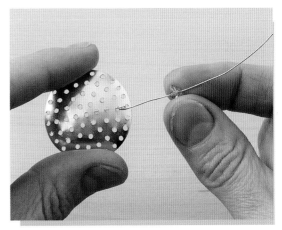

TIP:
This brooch is a great winter birthday gift option: Tanzanite is the birthstone for December, and amethyst is the birthstone for February!

1. Cut a 24" (60 cm) length of 26-gauge (0.4 mm) sterling silver wire using wire cutters. Insert 2" (5 cm) of one end of the wire through a hole in the second from outer ring of holes on top of the sieve. Insert the short end of the wire through a hole on the outer ring and "sew" the wire between the two holes twice to secure in place, using a pair of needle-nose pliers to pull the wire "stitches" tight. Snip off the excess wire under the sieve.

2. Thread a ¼" (6 mm) tanzanite spacer crystal bead onto the wire. Hold the bead 1¼" (3 cm) from the outer edge of the sieve.

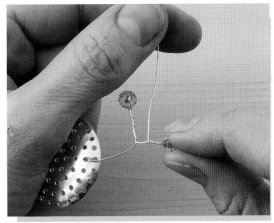

3. Cross the wire on itself under the bead, then twist the wires together for ½" (1.2 cm) under the bead.

4. Thread a ¼" (5 mm) violet faceted crystal bead onto the wire. Hold the bead ½" (1.2 cm) from the main wire. Cross the wire on itself under the bead, then twist the wires together until you reach the main wire.

5. Twist the two wires together until you reach the edge of the sieve. Bring the wire to the right side through the next hole in the second from outer ring of holes.

7. When you are close to running out of wire, sew the end of the wire twice between two holes in the sieve. Snip off the excess wire under the sieve. Repeat Step 1 to start the next length of wire and continue affixing wires and beads around the edge of the sieve.

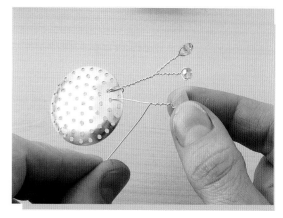

6. Thread on a blue lace agate chip. Hold the bead 1" (2.5 cm) from the outer edge of the sieve. Repeat Steps 2 to 5 to twist the wires and attach a mixture of tanzanite spacer crystal beads, violet faceted crystal beads, blue lace agate chips, rectangular amethyst beads, ¼" (5 mm) violet opal bicone crystal beads, ⅛" (4 mm) magenta freshwater pearls, and ⅛" (4 mm) mauve freshwater pearls, surrounding the sieve with the outer beads or chips 1¼" (3 cm) or 1" (2.5 cm) from the edge of the sieve.

VARIATION: *This pair of chunky clip-on earrings was made in the same way as the center of the starburst brooch. Freshwater pearl, crystal, and glass beads and semiprecious chips are sewn to a pair of small sieves that are attached with needle-nose pliers to clip-on earring backs.*

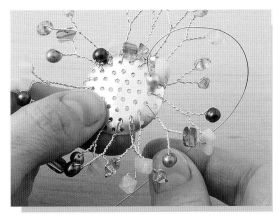

8. Bring the wire to the right side through one of the outer holes. Thread on a magenta potato freshwater pearl bead. Take the wire to the underside of the sieve and thread it through to the front through the next hole along on the outer ring of holes, then continue lacing beads and chips around the circumference of the sieve.

9. Bring the wire to the right side through an inner hole. Thread on a 5/16" (8 mm) baby blue side-drilled freshwater pearl bead. Insert the wire through the next hole. Repeat to sew a mixture of beads and chips in the middle of the sieve.

10. To finish, sew the wire twice between two holes. Cut off the excess wire on the underside of the sieve.

11. Place the sieve on the brooch back. Squeeze the prongs of the brooch back over the edge of the sieve with a pair of needle-nose pliers.

Woven Butterfly Ring

Sparkling butterfly-shaped crystals are a beautiful feature on this ring woven with crystal beads and freshwater pearls. Pacific opal crystal beads coordinate well with the turquoise pearls.

You Will Need

- 2 short beading needles
- Fine bead cord
- Approx. 11 x ¼" (5 mm) clear round faceted crystal beads
- Approx. 11 x ¼" (5mm) turquoise baroque freshwater pearls
- Approx. 11 x ¼" (5 mm) pacific opal round faceted crystal beads
- 12 x ⅛" (3 mm) clear bicone crystal beads
- 2 crystal butterflies
- Scissors

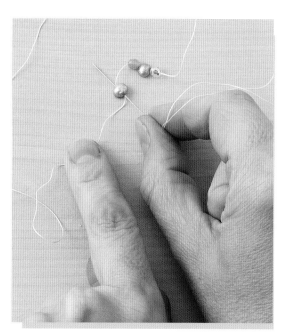

1. Thread a short beading needle with a 28" (70 cm) length of fine bead cord. Thread on a clear round faceted crystal bead, a turquoise baroque freshwater pearl, and a pacific opal round faceted crystal bead. Slide the round crystal beads and pearl to the center of the bead cord.

2. Thread on a pearl. Thread the other end of the bead cord onto a second needle. Insert the second needle through the second pearl, toward the threaded beads and pearl. Pull the bead cords tight, forming a ring of round crystal beads and pearls.

TIP:
Baroque pearls often have very small holes. Use a small beading needle to thread the beads.

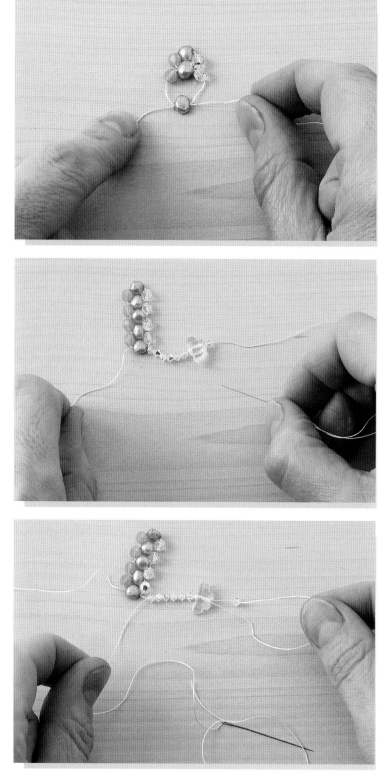

3. With the clear crystal bead on the right-hand side, thread a clear crystal bead and a pearl onto the right-hand bead cord and a pacific opal crystal bead onto the left-hand bead cord. Insert the left-hand needle through the last pearl.

4. Repeat Step 3 twice. Thread six ⅛" (3 mm) clear bicone crystal beads onto the right-hand bead cord. Insert the right-hand needle down through one crystal butterfly and one ⅛" (3 mm) clear bicone crystal bead.

5. Insert the needle back through the butterfly and the first six bicone crystals. Pull the bead cord to suspend the butterfly.

6. Repeat Step 3. Thread four bicone crystal beads, one crystal butterfly, and one bicone crystal bead onto the right-hand bead cord. Insert the needle back through the butterfly and first four bicone crystal beads. Pull the bead cord to suspend the butterfly. Repeat Step 3 four times.

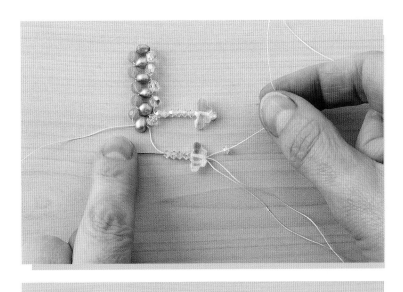

7. Thread a pacific opal crystal bead onto the left-hand bead cord. Thread a clear round crystal bead onto the right-hand bead cord.

8. Insert the left-hand bead cord through the first pearl. Pull the bead cords tight to form the ring.

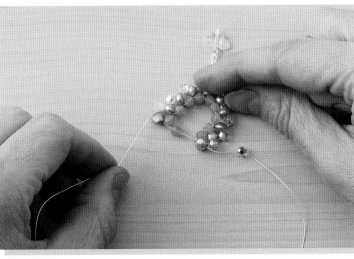

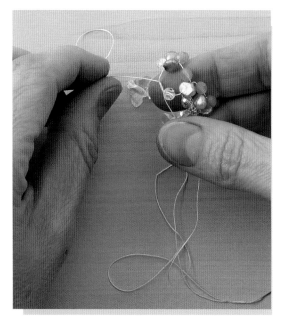 

9. Check the size of the ring. If you would like to enlarge it, slip the bead cord out of the first pearl and repeat Steps 3, 7, and 8. Knot the bead cords together in a double knot.

10. Weave the bead cords through the crystal beads and pearls. Cut off the excess bead cord with a pair of scissors.

VARIATION: *The bicone crystal beads and butterflies have been omitted from this lovely woven ring of black diamond crystal beads and coral baroque pearls.*

Chain and Bead Necklace

A chain necklace is always popular, and a few added beads will make it extra special. The soft colors of the chalcedony and fluorite beads used here blend together perfectly.

TIP:
Use the tip of a toothpick to dab a little clear nail polish on the joins of jump rings to secure them.

You Will Need

- 4 x ⅛" (4 mm) pacific opal round faceted crystal beads
- 3 x ⅜" (1 cm) chalcedony tumble beads
- 6 x ⅜" (1 cm) fluorite tumble beads
- 20" (50 cm) of 26-gauge (0.4 mm) gold-filled wire
- Needle-nose pliers
- Round-nose pliers
- 20" (50 cm) of ⅛" (2.5 mm)-wide gold-filled chain
- Wire cutters
- 11 x ⁵⁄₃₂" x ¼" (7 x 5 mm) gold-filled oval jump rings
- 5 x ⁵⁄₁₆" (8 mm) vermeil closed rings
- 3 x 1⅜" (3.5 cm) gold-filled ball pins
- 1 x ⅝" (1.5 cm) gold-filled S-hook clasp set

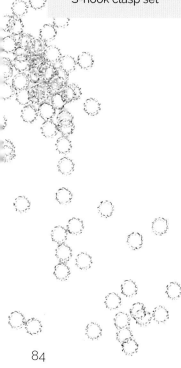

1. Refer to the technique on page 20 (Making Pinned Beads) to make individual pinned beads on 26-gauge (0.4 mm) gold-filled wire with the following beads: four ⅛" (4 mm) pacific opal round faceted crystal beads, two ⅜" (1 cm) chalcedony tumble beads, and five ⅜" (1 cm) fluorite tumble beads.

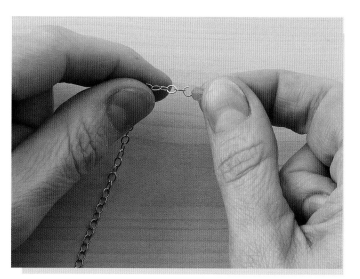

2. Cut a 5⅝" (14.5 cm) length of ⅛" (2.5 mm)-wide gold-filled chain with wire cutters. Open one loop of a pinned pacific opal crystal bead. Slip one end of the chain onto the loop. Close the loop using two pairs of pliers.

3. Open two ⁵/₃₂" x ¼"
(7 x 5 mm) gold-filled
oval jump rings. Slip
the other loop of the
pinned pacific opal
bead and one ⁵/₁₆"
(8 mm) vermeil closed
ring onto one jump ring.
Close the jump ring.

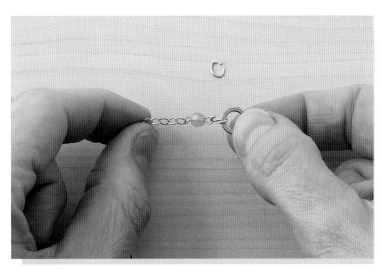

4. Link a pinned
chalcedony tumble
bead between two
pinned fluorite tumble
beads, referring to the
technique on page 20
(Making Pinned Beads).
Slip the vermeil closed
ring and the top loop of
the linked chalcedony
and fluorite beads onto
the other jump ring.
Close the jump ring.

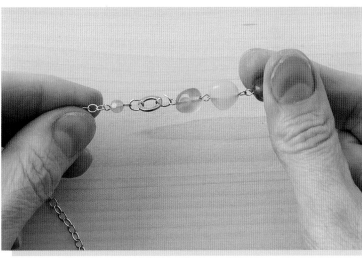

5. Cut a 1¼" (3 cm) length
of chain with wire
cutters. Open the lower
loop of the linked
chalcedony and fluorite
beads. Slip one end
of the chain onto the
loop. Close the loop.
Repeat Steps 2 to 5 to
make the other side of
the necklace.

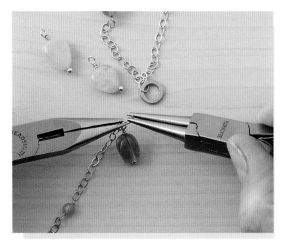

6. Open another jump ring. Slip both ends of the short chain and a vermeil closed ring onto the jump ring. Close the jump ring.

7. Cut a ⅝" (1.5 cm) and a 1¼" (3 cm) length of chain with wire cutters. Affix a pinned pacific opal crystal bead between the lengths of chain. Refer to the technique on page 19 (Making a Wrapped Loop) to secure a fluorite tumble bead and two chalcedony tumble beads on ball pins. Open a jump ring. Slip the end of the longer chain and the wrapped fluorite bead onto the jump ring. Close the jump ring.

8. Cut two 1¼" (3 cm) lengths of chain with wire cutters. Affix a pinned pacific opal crystal bead between the lengths of chain. Open a jump ring. Slip one end of the chain and a wrapped chalcedony bead onto the jump ring. Close the jump ring.

9. Cut two ¾" (2 cm) lengths of chain with wire cutters. Affix a pinned fluorite bead between the lengths of chain. Open a jump ring. Slip one end of the chain and a wrapped chalcedony bead onto the jump ring. Close the jump ring.

10. Open a jump ring. Slip the lower vermeil closed ring and the top of the three "hanging" chains onto the jump ring. Close the jump ring.

11. Open a jump ring. Slip the end of the chain on one side of the necklace and the S-hook onto the jump ring. Close the jump ring. Repeat to affix the ring of the S-hook clasp set to the other end of the necklace.

VARIATION: *This sterling silver chain has pinned ¼" (5 mm) coral pink glass and ⁵⁄₁₆" (8mm) peach freshwater pearls anchored with a hammered sterling silver closed oval ring.*

Chain Drop Earrings

The five-hole end bars used to suspend sparkling crystal beads on these dramatic earrings are usually associated with multistrand necklaces and bracelets, but they are also great for hanging beads on earrings. Short lengths of chain suspend more crystal and pearl beads to create an elaborate chandelier style.

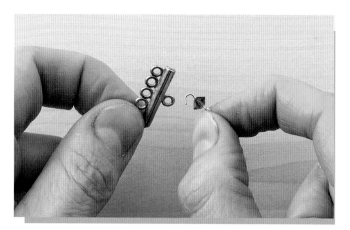

1. Refer to the technique on page 20 (Making Pinned Beads) to affix a ¼" (6 mm) dark aqua spacer crystal bead on a gold-filled eye pin. Open one loop of the pinned bead and slip it onto the top ring of a gold-filled five-hole end bar. Close the loop using two pairs of pliers.

2. Slip a tanzanite faceted crystal drop bead onto a 3⅛" (8 cm) length of 26-gauge (0.4 mm) gold-filled wire with ¾" (2 cm) of the wire extending on one side. Pull the wires tightly across the top of the bead.

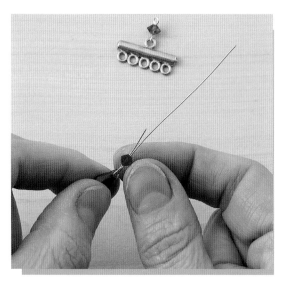

3. Use a pair of needle-nose pliers to bend each wire upwards at the point where the two wires cross. Thread a ⅛" (4 mm) siam bicone crystal bead onto both wires.

4. Snip the short end of wire ⅛" (3 mm) above the top of the siam bead with wire cutters. Refer to Steps 3 to 6 of the technique on page 21 (Making a Wrapped Side- or Top-Drilled Bead) to finish wrapping the beads.

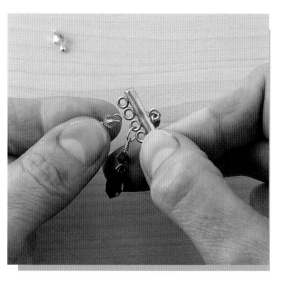

5. Open a 5⁄32" x ¼" (7 x 5 mm) gold-filled oval jump ring. Slip the loop of the wrapped beads and the center ring of the five-hole end bar onto the jump ring. Close the jump ring using two pairs of pliers.

6. Refer to the technique on page 18 (Making a Single Loop) to affix two ⅛" (4 mm) light sapphire bicone crystal beads on 1⅜" (3.5 cm) gold-filled ball pins. Open the loops and hang these on the second and fourth rings of the end bar.

7. Refer to the technique on page 20 (Making Pinned Beads) to affix a dark aqua spacer crystal bead and a ⅛" x ¼" (3 x 5 mm) white rondelle freshwater pearl on an eye pin. Repeat to make another pinned bead. Open the loop above the dark aqua crystal beads and slip them onto the first and last rings in the end bar. Close the loops using two pairs of pliers.

8. Open the loops under the pearl beads. Cut two ½" (1.2 cm) lengths of ⅛" (2.5 mm)-wide gold-filled chain with wire cutters. Hang one end of the chains onto the loops. Close the loops using two pairs of pliers.

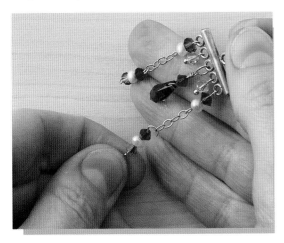

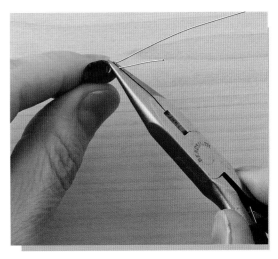

9. Refer to the technique on page 20 (Making Pinned Beads) to affix a siam bicone crystal bead, a white rondelle freshwater pearl, and a ⅙" (4 mm) amethyst bicone crystal bead on an eye pin. Repeat to make another pinned bead. Open the loop above the siam beads and hook these onto the ends of the chains. Close the loops.

10. Slip a ⅜" (1 cm) siam crystal heart onto a 3⅛" (8 cm) length of wire with ¾" (2 cm) of the wire extending on one side. Pull the wires tightly across the top of the heart. Use a pair of needle-nose pliers to bend each wire upwards at the point where the two wires cross. Thread a dark aqua spacer crystal bead and a light sapphire bicone crystal bead onto both wires.

11. Snip the short end of wire ⅛" (3 mm) above the top of the siam bead with wire cutters. Refer to Steps 3 to 6 of the technique on page 21 (Making a Wrapped Side- or Top-Drilled Bead) to finish wrapping the beads. Open the loops under the pinned amethyst beads. Hook the loop at the top of the wrapped beads onto the loops of the pinned beads. Close the loops.

12. Open a jump ring. Slip the eye of a gold-filled hook earring wire and the loop of the pinned dark aqua bead onto the jump ring. Close the jump ring using two pairs of pliers. Make a matching earring.

VARIATION: *Here is an elegant pair of chain drop earrings. Wrapped turquoise and crystal hearts and ⅛" (4 mm) black diamond bicone crystal beads hang on jump rings from 1½" (4 cm) and 1" (2.5 cm) lengths of chain.*

Three-Strand Choker

This dramatic choker of stunning crystals is just the thing for a glamorous event. Three rows of crystal beads in coordinating colors are secured through three-hole spacer bars and hung with beautiful faceted crystal hearts.

You Will Need

- 2 x ⅛" (4 mm) sterling silver jump rings
- 1 sterling silver clasp
- 2 sterling silver three-hole end bars
- 4 sterling silver three-hole spacer bars
- 70" (175 cm) flexible beading wire
- Wire cutters

- Masking tape
- Approx. 80 x ⅛" (4 mm) light sapphire bicone crystal beads
- Approx. 80 x ⅛" (4 mm) sapphire bicone crystal beads
- Approx. 160 x ⅛" (4 mm) amethyst AB2X bicone crystal beads
- 24" (60 cm) of 26-gauge (0.4 mm) sterling silver wire

- 4 x ⅜" (1 cm) sapphire crystal hearts
- 2 x ¹¹⁄₁₆" (1.7 cm) amethyst AB2X crystal hearts
- 2 x ⅜" (1 cm) light sapphire crystal hearts
- Needle-nose pliers
- Round-nose pliers
- 8 sterling silver crimp beads
- Crimping pliers

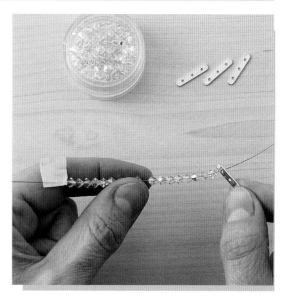

1. Decide the finished length you wish the choker to be. Affix jump rings to the clasp, then to the end bars. Measure the width of the end bars with the jump rings and clasp between them. Measure the depth of the four spacer bars. Take both these measurements off the finished choker length. Divide this final measurement by five.

2. Cut three 18" (45 cm) lengths of flexible beading wire using wire cutters. Wrap a piece of masking tape 3" (7.5 cm) from one end of each length to keep the beads from slipping off. Thread ⅛" (4 mm) light sapphire bicone crystal beads for the one-fifth measurement (from Step 1) onto one of the lengths. You will need an even number of beads for each of the five sections of the choker. If necessary, thread on fewer beads rather than more to achieve an even number. Thread the beading wire through the top hole of a spacer bar.

3. Continue threading on light sapphire bicone crystal beads until you have five equal sections of beads with spacer bars between them. Wrap a piece of masking tape around the beading wire after the last bead.

4. On the second length of beading wire, repeat to thread on ⅛" (4 mm) sapphire bicone crystal beads in the same way, but threading the beading wire through the center hole of the spacer bars.

5. Thread the required number of ⅛" (4 mm) amethyst AB2X bicone crystal beads onto the third beading wire. Insert the beading wire through the lower hole of the first spacer bar. Thread on half the required number of bicone beads for the next section. Refer to the technique on page 21 (Making a Wrapped Side- or Top-Drilled Bead) to make a loop on the heart crystal beads using 0.4 mm sterling silver wire.

6. Thread a sapphire crystal heart onto the beading wire, then half the required number of bicone beads. Insert the beading wire through the lower hole of the second spacer bar. Thread on half the required number of bicone beads for the next section. Thread on a ¹¹⁄₁₆" (1.7 cm) amethyst AB2X crystal heart. Finish the second half of the third row to match the first half.

7. Cut a 16" (40 cm) length of beading wire. Insert one end through a crimp bead and the lower hole of the first spacer bar. Insert 1½" (4 cm) of the beading wire back through the crimp bead and pull the beading wire tight, allowing for some movement. Secure the crimp bead using a pair of crimping pliers, referring to the technique on page 22 (Using a Crimp Bead). Snip off the excess beading wire with wire cutters.

8. Thread on thirteen amethyst AB2X bicone crystal beads, one light sapphire crystal heart, and eleven amethyst AB2X bicone crystal beads. Insert the beading wire through the lower hole of the second spacer bar and down through the last bicone bead. Pull the beading wire tight.

9. Thread on ten amethyst AB2X bicone crystal beads, one sapphire crystal heart, four black diamond AB bicone crystal beads, one black diamond AB crystal heart, four black diamond AB bicone crystal beads, one sapphire crystal heart, and eleven amethyst AB2X bicone crystal beads. Insert the beading wire through the lower hole of the third spacer bar and down through the last bicone bead. Pull the beading wire tight.

10. Thread on ten amethyst AB2X bicone crystal beads, one light sapphire crystal heart, thirteen amethyst AB2X bicone crystal beads, and a crimp bead. Insert the beading wire through the lower hole of the fourth spacer bar and down through the crimp bead. Secure the crimp bead using a pair of crimping pliers. Snip off the excess wire with wire cutters.

11. Remove the masking tape. Check the length of the choker, allowing space for the end bars, jump rings, and clasp. Add more beads at each end if needed. Insert one end of the top beading wire through a crimp bead and the top ring of one end bar. Insert the end of the beading wire back through the crimp bead, suspending the end bars and necklace fastening.

12. Secure the crimp bead using a pair of crimping pliers. Snip off the excess beading wire with wire cutters. Repeat on the second and third beading wire. Push the beads and spacer bars along the beading wires. Affix the other end of the beading wires to the other end bar with crimp beads as before.

VARIATION: *This pretty bracelet has two three-hole spacer bars between three strands of beautiful freshwater pearls in natural colors. When working out the length of the strands, divide the final measurement by three instead of five as described in Step 1.*

Multistrand Bracelet

This elaborate bracelet has five strands of assorted semiprecious beads in soft, coordinating colors. The strands are anchored through five-hole spacer bars and finished with end caps.

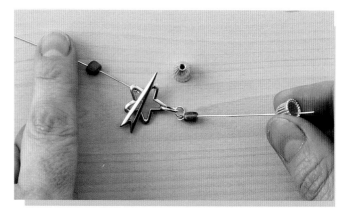

1. To calculate the length of the bracelet, slip the eye of each eye pin onto a ⅛" (4 mm) jump ring. Affix the jump rings onto the ring on each side of a toggle clasp using two pairs of pliers. Fasten the clasp. Thread one purple square cat's-eye bead and an end cap onto each eye pin.

2. Lay the piece flat and measure the length. Subtract this measurement from the desired bracelet length. Use wire cutters to cut five lengths of flexible beading wire 4" (10 cm) longer than the final measurement. Remove the eye pins and set the cat's-eye beads and end caps aside.

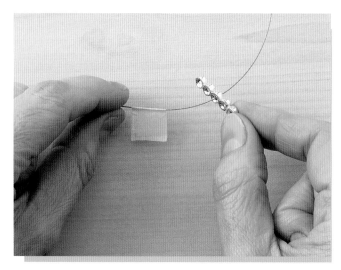

3. Wrap a piece of masking tape around one end of each beading wire 1½" (4 cm) from one end to keep the beads from slipping off. Insert the first beading wire through the center hole of a five-hole sterling silver spacer bar.

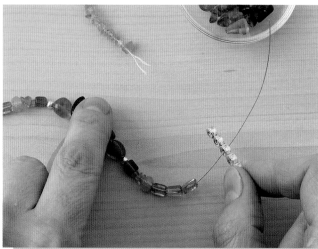

4. Thread on three ¼" x ⅛" (6 x 4 mm) rectangular amethyst beads, one ⁵⁄₁₆" (8 mm) pacific opal faceted rondelle, apatite chips for ¼" (5 mm), one purple square cat's-eye bead, one ⅛" (3 mm) sterling silver bead, one ⅜" (1 cm) fluorite tumble bead, one amethyst chip, and one ⅜" (1 cm) chalcedony tumble bead. The ⅜" (1 cm) chalcedony tumble bead will be the center of the bracelet. Bead the other half of the beading wire to match the first half. Thread the beading wire through the center hole of the other spacer bar.

5. Remove the masking tape. Thread equal amounts of apatite chips at each end of the beading wire until the beaded beading wire is the required measurement. Tape one end of the beading wire to keep the beads from slipping off.

6. Thread on a crimp bead and eye pin. Insert the beading wire back through the crimp bead, leaving a small loop of beading wire through the eye pin that allows for some movement.

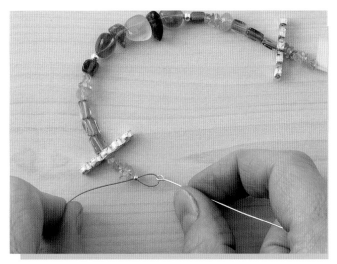

7. Refer to the technique on page 22 (Using a Crimp Bead) to secure the crimp bead in place using a pair of crimping pliers. Snip off the excess beading wire with wire cutters. Push the beads and chips along the beading wire to the eye pin. Remove the tape and repeat to secure the other end to an eye pin with a crimp bead.

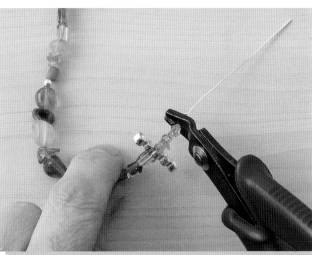

8. Tape one eye pin to your work surface to hold the bracelet steady. At the taped end, insert a beading wire through the next hole on the spacer bar. Repeat Step 4, checking that the center bead and spacer bars are parallel. Add more apatite chips to keep the beads level if necessary.

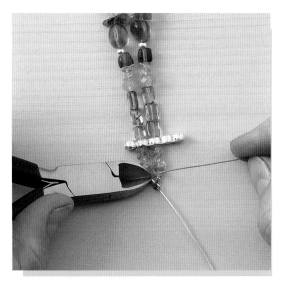

9. Remove the tape at the start of the beading wire. Thread on apatite chips. You will need more apatite chips than on the first beading wire to allow for the outer strand leaning in to meet the eye pin. Thread on a crimp bead. Insert the beading wire through the eye of the eye pin, then back through the crimp bead, leaving a small loop of beading wire through the eye pin that allows for some movement. Secure the crimp bead in place as before with a pair of crimping pliers. Repeat at the other end of the beading wire.

10. Working outwards from the center, bead and secure the other beading wires between the eye pins. Thread an end cap onto one eye pin. It will cover the crimped ends of the beading wire. Thread on one purple square cat's-eye bead. Refer to the technique on page 19 (Making a Wrapped Loop) to make a wrapped loop above the bead. Repeat on the other end of the bracelet.

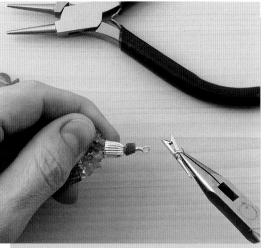

VARIATION: *Lovely shades of pink combine on this multistrand bracelet of pearls, glass foil-lined beads, rock crystal chips, rose quartz chips, opaque glass beads, and tourmaline chips.*

11. Use two pairs of pliers to open a jump ring on the clasp. Slip the loop of one wrapped loop onto the jump ring. Close the jump ring using the pliers. Repeat at the other end of the bracelet.

Tied Flower Lariat

At about one yard (90 cm) long, this charming lariat can be worn in a variety of ways. Subtly colored velvet flowers are interspersed along the lariat among beads and pearls of coordinating colors.

TIP:
When tying jump rings and loops of the flowers to the bead cord, position the flowers toward the ends of the bead cord.

You Will Need

- 43 assorted crystal, glass, freshwater pearl, and jade beads ranging from ¼" (5 mm) to ¾" (2 cm) in shades of amber, green, light blue, and gray
- Approx. 41 x 1⅜" (3.5 cm) gold-filled ball pins
- Approx. 7 x 2" (5 cm) gold-filled ball pins
- Needle-nose pliers
- Round-nose pliers
- 8 x ¾" (2 cm) pale blue and fawn velvet flowers
- 4 x ¼" (5 mm) black diamond round faceted crystal beads
- 14 x ⁵⁄₁₆" (8 mm) sterling silver jump rings
- Wire cutters
- Light blue no. 12 carded bead cord
- Cyanoacrylate adhesive
- Scissors

1. Slip the assorted crystal, freshwater pearl, glass, and jade beads onto ball pins; use 1⅜" (3.5 cm) ball pins for the smaller beads and 2" (5 cm) ball pins for larger or longer beads. If the glass beads have large holes, thread on a crystal bead first. Refer to the technique on page 19 (Making a Wrapped Loop) to affix the beads using two pairs of pliers.

2. Carefully pull or cut the flower heads off their stems and remove the stamens. Slip a ¼" (5 mm) black diamond round faceted crystal bead onto four 1⅜" (3.5 cm) ball pins. With wrong sides facing, thread two flowers onto each ball pin.

3. Snip the wire ⅜" (1 cm) above the last flower using wire cutters. Hold the end of the ball pin with a pair of round-nose pliers ⅛" (3 mm) from the tip of the jaws. Bend the wire toward you to make a loop that is centered over the flower. Repeat on all the ball pins.

4. Set one large bead aside. Open the jump rings using two pairs of pliers. Slip the wrapped loops of two large beads or three small beads onto each jump ring. Close the jump rings using two pairs of pliers.

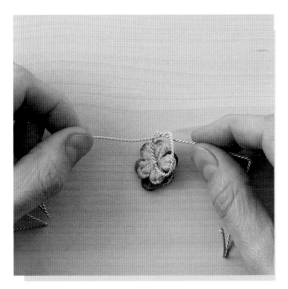

5. Slip the loop of one flower onto a 53" (135 cm) length of light blue no. 12 bead cord. Tie the loop to the cord 6" (15 cm) from one end.

6. Set one jump ring and one flower aside. Slip the other jump rings and loops of the flowers onto the cord, tying them in place at 2" (5 cm) intervals.

7. Slip the set-aside flower and large bead onto the bead cord and tie them to the cord with a double knot 2" (5 cm) after the last jump ring.

8. Slip the set-aside jump ring of beads onto the other end of the bead cord and tie them to the cord with a double knot 2" (5 cm) after the flower.

9. Dab the end knots with glue and leave to dry. Cut off the excess cord close to the end knots with a pair of scissors.

VARIATION: *Here is a delicately colored lariat of cream flowers, pale green and cream pearls, violet crystal beads, amethyst beads, blue lace agate chips, and mother-of-pearl disks.*

Ladder Bracelet

Simple bead weaving is used to make this beautiful bracelet. A fabulous ladder effect is achieved by using long-drilled freshwater pearl beads bordered with button top-drilled pearls.

You Will Need

- ¼" (6 mm) round sterling silver ball clasp
- 2 x ¼" (5 mm) sterling silver jump rings
- 2 sterling silver clamshell crimps
- Round-nose pliers
- Needle-nose pliers
- Fine bead cord
- Scissors
- Masking tape
- 2 long beading needles
- Approx. 52 x ⁵⁄₁₆" (7mm) lilac button top-drilled freshwater pearl beads
- Approx. 20 x 1" (2.5cm) peacock long-drilled freshwater pearl beads
- Cyanoacrylate adhesive

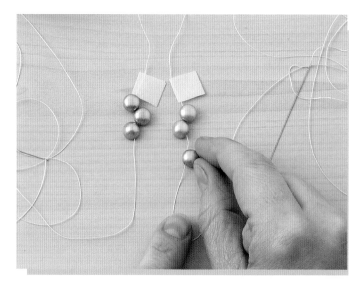

1. To calculate the length of the bracelet, slip a jump ring onto each end of the clasp. Slip a clamshell crimp onto each jump ring. Close the jump ring using two pairs of pliers. Lay the piece out flat and measure the length. For the final measurement, subtract this measurement plus 1¼" (3 cm) from the desired bracelet length. Remove the clamshell crimps.

2. Cut two 48" (120 cm) lengths of fine bead cord. Wrap a piece of masking tape around the bead cords 6" (15 cm) from one end to keep the beads from slipping off. Thread a long beading needle onto each bead cord. Thread three lilac button top-drilled freshwater pearl beads onto each bead cord.

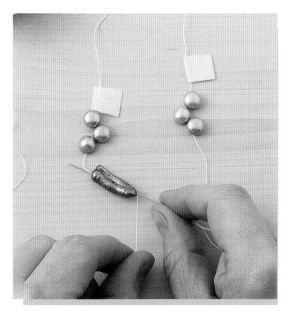

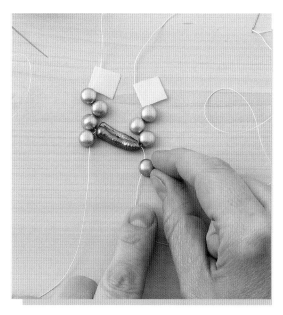

3. Thread a peacock long-drilled freshwater pearl bead onto one bead cord. Insert the other bead cord through the long-drilled bead in the other direction.

4. Thread a button bead onto each bead cord, keeping the top-drilled edge of the bead toward the long-drilled bead.

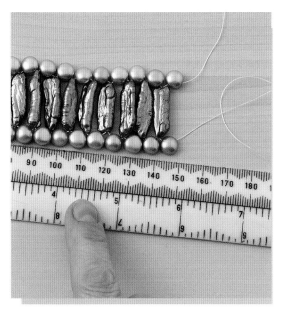

5. Repeat Steps 3 and 4 until the bracelet measures the final measurement described in Step 1 between the centers of the first and last long-drilled beads.

6. Thread two lilac button top-drilled freshwater pearl beads onto each bead cord. Insert both bead cords through the hole in a clamshell crimp.

7. Remove the masking tape at the start of the bracelet and insert both bead cords through the hole in a clamshell crimp. Tie the bead cords securely together in a double knot over the hole of the clamshell crimp. Cut off the excess bead cord close to the knots.

8. Dab cyanoacrylate adhesive on the knots to secure them in place. Close the cups of the clamshell crimps with a pair of needle-nose pliers.

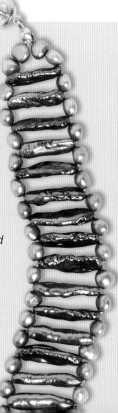

VARIATION:
This copper-colored bracelet has long-drilled freshwater pearls graduated in size so the longest beads are concentrated in the center. The bracelet is bordered with baroque freshwater pearls and fastens with gold-filled findings.

9. Slip a clamshell crimp onto each jump ring on the clasp. Close the jump rings using two pairs of pliers.

Twisted Necklace

If you have a feature pendant, this necklace is a great way of showing it off. Twist the necklace a few times before you wear it—the tighter the strings of beads are twisted, the shorter the necklace will be. The necklace fastens with an extension chain so the length can be further adjusted.

TIP:
A twisted necklace also looks great without a pendant.

You Will Need

- 72" (180 cm) flexible beading wire
- Masking tape
- 28 x ⅛" (3 mm) round hematite beads
- 26 x ½" (1.2 cm) hematite cylindrical beads
- 7 sterling silver crimp beads
- 2 sterling silver eye pins

- Crimping pliers
- Wire cutters
- Approx. 114 x ⅛" (4 mm) light green pressed glass beads
- Approx. 69 x ¼" (6 mm) round rock crystal beads
- 2 x ⅜" (1 cm) Bali-style sterling silver end caps
- 4 x ⅛" (4 mm) sterling silver jump rings

- Needle-nose pliers
- Round-nose pliers
- 1 sterling silver lobster claw clasp
- 1 x 1⅜" (3.5 cm) sterling silver ball pin
- Sterling silver extension chain
- Handmade glass pendant

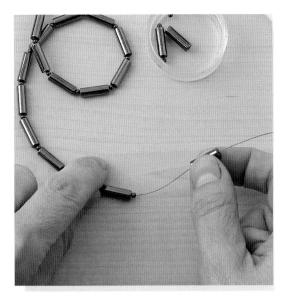

1. Wrap a piece of masking tape around the end of a 25" (55 cm) length of flexible beading wire to keep the beads from slipping off. Thread a sequence of a ⅛" (3 mm) round hematite bead and a ½" (1.2 cm) hematite cylindrical bead twenty-six times onto the beading wire. Thread on another ⅛" (3 mm) round hematite bead.

2. Insert the end of the beading wire through a crimp bead and the eye of an eye pin. Insert the beading wire back through the crimp bead and pull the end of the wire to tighten the loop of the wire through the eye pin.

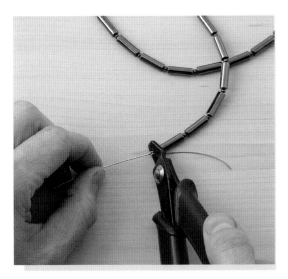

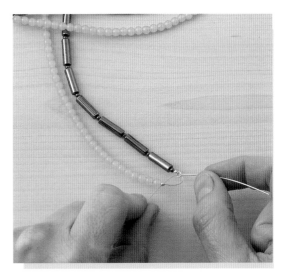

3. Refer to the technique on page 22 (Using a Crimp Bead) to secure the crimp bead with a pair of crimping pliers. Snip off the excess beading wire with a pair of wire cutters. Repeat at the other end of the beading wire.

4. Thread ⅛" (4 mm) light green pressed glass beads onto beading wire until the beads are the same length as the hematite beads. Secure the beaded beading wire to the eye pins with crimp beads as before.

5. Thread ¼" (6 mm) round rock crystal beads onto beading wire until the beads are the same length as the hematite beads. Secure the beaded beading wire to the eye pins with crimp beads as before.

6. Insert one eye pin through an end cap and two green pressed glass beads. Refer to the technique on page 19 (Making a Wrapped Loop) to make a wrapped loop above the last bead. Repeat at the other end of the necklace.

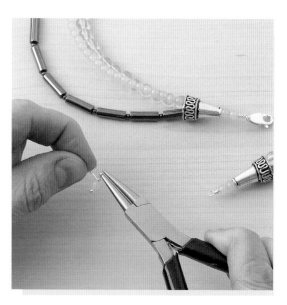

7. Open a ⅛" (4 mm) sterling silver jump ring. Slip a lobster claw clasp and the loop of the wrapped loop onto the jump ring. Close the jump ring using two pairs of pliers.

8. Slip a green pressed glass bead onto a 1⅜" (3.5 cm) sterling silver ball pin. Refer to the technique on page 19 (Making a Wrapped Loop) to make a wrapped loop above the bead.

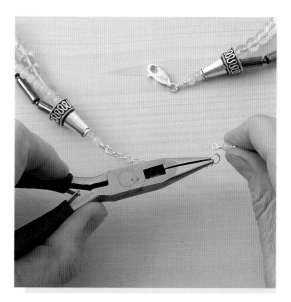

9. Open a jump ring. Slip the loop of the wrapped bead and one end of the extension chain onto the ring. Close the ring using two pairs of pliers.

10. Open another jump ring. Slip the loop of the wrapped bead and the end of the chain onto the jump ring. Close the ring using two pairs of pliers.

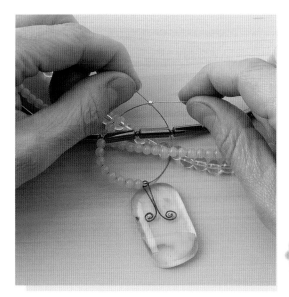

11. Thread a handmade glass pendant facing forward, ten green pressed glass beads, and a crimp bead onto a 5¼" (13 cm) length of beading wire. Wrap the beading wire around the necklace and insert the other end through the crimp bead.

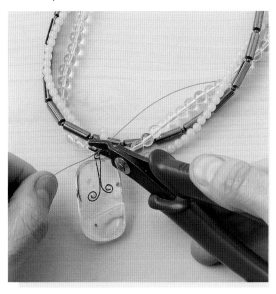

12. Pull the beading wire tight and secure the crimp bead with a pair of crimping pliers. Snip off the excess beading wire.

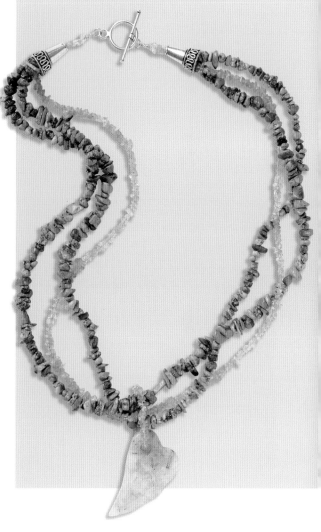

VARIATION: *Two strings of turquoise chips and one of delicate apatite chips are twisted together and suspend a fabulous tourmalinated green quartz heart pendant.*

Rosette Brooch

The glorious flower effect of this stunning brooch is achieved by sewing petal-shaped or drop beads in concentric circles to a metal sieve. The beads used must be side-drilled across one end so they can be sewn with fine wire.

You Will Need

- Approx. 48" (120 cm) of 26-gauge (0.4 mm) sterling silver wire
- Wire cutters
- 1 x 1¼" (3 cm) silver-colored brooch back and sieve
- Needle-nose pliers
- Approx. 24 x 1¼" (3 cm) dyed gray petal-shaped mother-of-pearl side-drilled beads
- 1 x 2" (5 cm) sterling silver head pin
- Round-nose pliers

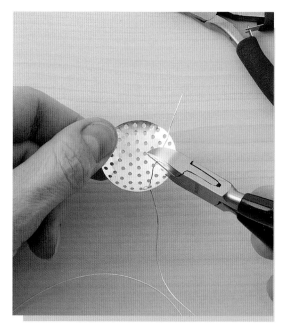

1. Cut a 24" (60 cm) length of 26-gauge (0.4 mm) sterling silver wire. Insert 2" (5 cm) of one end of the wire down through a hole in the outer ring of holes in the sieve. Bring the end to the right side through the next hole to the left. Repeat to secure the wire in place.

2. Use a pair of needle-nose pliers to pull the wire "stitches" tight. Snip off the excess wire under the sieve.

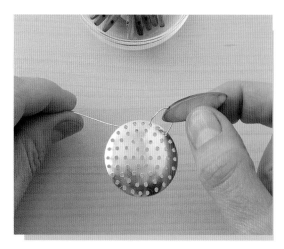

3. Thread a 1¼" (3 cm) petal-shaped mother-of-pearl dyed gray side-drilled bead onto the wire. Slip the bead down the wire. Insert the wire through the second hole to the left, positioning the bead over the anchored wire with the bead pointing outwards. Pull the wire tight.

4. Bring the wire to the right side, four holes to the right-hand side. Thread on a petal bead. Insert the wire through the second hole to the left. Pull the wire tight.

5. Repeat Step 4 to affix beads all around the outer ring of holes, using a pair of needle-nose pliers to pull the wire tight as you work. When you are close to running out of wire, sew the end of the wire twice between two holes in the sieve. Snip off the excess wire under the sieve. Repeat Step 1 to continue with the next length of wire.

6. Bring the wire to the right side through a hole in the second ring of holes. Thread on a petal bead. Insert the wire through the second hole to the left. Pull the wire tight. Bring the wire to the right side, four holes to the right-hand side. Repeat to affix petal beads all around the second ring of holes.

7. Bring the wire to the right side through a hole in the third ring of holes. Thread on a petal bead. Insert the wire through the second hole to the left. Pull the wire tight. Bring the wire to the right side, four holes to the right-hand side. Repeat to affix petal beads all around the third ring of holes.

8. Bring the wire to the right side through any empty hole. Insert the wire to the wrong side through the next hole. Repeat to secure the wire in place. Use a pair of needle-nose pliers to pull the wire tight. Snip off the excess wire under the sieve.

9. Thread a ⁵⁄₁₆" (8 mm) round jet bead onto a 2" (5 cm) sterling silver head pin. Insert the head pin down through the center of the sieve.

10. Snip the wire of the head pin ⅜" (1 cm) below the sieve with a pair of wire cutters.

11. Bend the extending wire into a loop with a pair of round-nose pliers. Lay the loop flat against the underside of the sieve.

12. Place the sieve on the brooch back. Squeeze the prongs of the brooch back over the edge of the sieve with a pair of needle-nose pliers.

VARIATION:
This pretty ring has sapphire blue glass spear-shaped beads affixed to a small sieve and ring back. An amethyst bead sits at the center.

Cluster Stud Earrings

Crystals and pearls in autumnal shades combine on this delightful pair of stud earrings. The tiny beads are affixed to ball pins and cluster on each earring around a large glass pearl threaded on an eye pin.

You Will Need

- 2 x ⅛" (4 mm) light rose bicone crystal beads
- 2 x ⅛" (4 mm) black diamond bicone crystal beads
- 6 x ⅛" (4mm) light gold rondelle freshwater pearl beads
- 24 x 1⅜" (3.5 cm) gold-filled ball pins

- Round-nose pliers
- Needle-nose pliers
- Wire cutters
- 2 x ½" (1.2 cm) copper-colored glass pearl beads
- 2 x 2" (5 cm) gold-filled eye pins
- 4 x ¼" (6mm) coral potato freshwater pearl beads

- 8 x ¼" (6 mm) light colorado faceted rondelle crystal beads
- 2 x ⅛" (4 mm) rose bicone crystal beads
- 2 x ⅛" (4 mm) topaz bicone crystal beads
- 2 gold-filled earring studs with rings

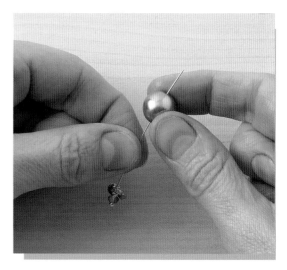

1. Slip a ⅛" (4 mm) light rose bicone crystal bead, a ⅛" (4 mm) black diamond bicone crystal bead, and a light gold rondelle freshwater pearl onto three 1⅜" (3.5 cm) gold-filled ball pins. Refer to the technique on page 19 (Making a Wrapped Loop) to make a wrapped loop above each bead.

2. Open the eye of a 2" (5 cm) gold-filled eye pin using two pairs of pliers. Slip the loops of the wrapped beads onto the eye. Close the eye with two pairs of pliers. Thread a ½" (1.2 cm) copper-colored glass pearl bead onto the eye pin.

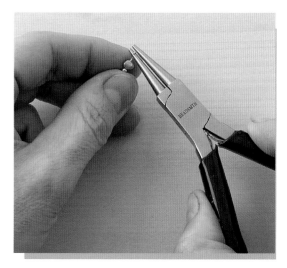

3. Slip two coral potato freshwater pearl beads and three ¼" (6 mm) light colorado faceted rondelle crystal beads onto five 1⅜" (3.5 cm) gold-filled ball pins. Refer to the technique on page 19 (Making a Wrapped Loop) to make a wrapped loop above each bead. Thread the wrapped beads onto the eye pin.

4. Slip a ⅛" (4 mm) rose bicone crystal bead, a ⅛" (4 mm) topaz bicone crystal bead, and two light gold rondelle freshwater pearls onto four 1⅜" (3.5 cm) gold-filled ball pins. Refer to the technique on page 18 (Making a Single Loop) to make a single loop above each bead.

5. Thread the beads onto the eye pin. Holding the eye pin upright, splay the beads outwards from the eye pin. Thread a light colorado faceted rondelle crystal bead onto the eye pin.

6. Refer to the technique on page 19 (Making a Wrapped Loop) to make a wrapped loop above the bead, wrapping the wire tightly around the eye pin to press the rondelle crystal bead down onto the loops of wire.

7. Carefully open the ring on the earring stud with a pair of pliers. Slip the wrapped loop onto the ring. Close the ring using the pliers. Make a matching earring.

VARIATION: *The soft green and white color scheme gives a summery feel to this pair of charming earrings. Each earring has a ⅝" (1.5 cm) white glass pearl threaded on a sterling silver ball pin. Triangular peridot beads and opalite chips with wrapped loops are threaded on and topped with mother-of-pearl and opalite chips.*

Hoop Earrings

Plain hoop earrings have been jazzed up with hanging apatite chips to achieve a fabulous bohemian style. The earrings are simple to make, with sterling silver disks hanging among the chips on ball pins.

You Will Need

- Masking tape
- Round-nose pliers
- 10 x ⁵⁄₁₆" (8 mm) sterling silver disks
- 50 apatite smooth chips
- 30 x 2" (5 cm) sterling silver ball pins
- 2 sterling silver hoop earrings
- Needle-nose pliers
- Wire cutters

1. Stick a strip of masking tape around one jaw of a pair of round-nose pliers ⅛" (4 mm) from the tip. This will help to keep the loop you make on the ball pins that suspend the chips large enough to slip onto the earring hoops.

2. Thread a ⁵⁄₁₆" (8 mm) sterling silver disk and five apatite smooth chips onto a 2" (5 cm) sterling silver ball pin. If the smooth chips you have are graduated in size, use the largest for this ball pin, as it will be at the center of the hoop. Set aside five of the largest chips for the center of the other earring.

3. Refer to the technique on page 19 (Making a Wrapped Loop) to make a wrapped loop above the chips, placing the loop at the ⅛" (4 mm) position on the round-nose pliers.

4. Slip the loop onto a hoop. Close the hoop and hold it at the top so the chips hang down from the center. Gently squeeze the loop around the hoop with a pair of needle-nose pliers to secure the ball pin in place.

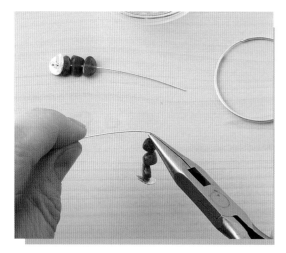

5. Thread a sterling silver disk and three apatite smooth chips onto two ball pins. Make a wrapped loop above the chips as before. Thread the loops onto the hoop on each side of the first loop. Gently squeeze the loops around the hoop with a pair of needle-nose pliers to secure the ball pin in place as before, positioning the loops ⅛" (3 mm) apart.

6. Thread a sterling silver disk and two apatite smooth chips onto two ball pins. Make a wrapped loop above the chips as before. Thread the loops onto the hoop on each side of the three hanging loops. Gently squeeze the loops around the hoop with a pair of needle-nose pliers to secure the ball pin in place as before.

VARIATION: *The green aventurine triangular beads look very elegant on this pair of gold-filled hoops. Two beads are threaded on the center ball pin with four single beads suspended on each side.*

7. Thread an apatite smooth chip onto ten ball pins. Make a wrapped loop above each chip as before. Thread five loops onto the hoop on each side of the fixed hanging loops. Gently squeeze the loops around the hoop with a pair of needle-nose pliers to secure the ball pin in place as before. Make a matching earring.

Spiral Ring

This attention-demanding ring is created using a variety of techniques. The dramatic wire coils are simple to make. Plastic-tipped pliers, which will not mark the wire, are used to hold the wire while you work.

You Will Need

- Approx. 4¾" (12 cm) of 26-gauge (0.4 mm) sterling silver wire
- Needle-nose pliers
- Round-nose pliers
- Wire cutters

- 1 x ¾" x ⅝" (1.8 x 1.5 cm) amethyst faceted hexagonal crystal bead
- 6¼" (16 cm) of 31-gauge (1 mm) sterling silver wire
- Jewelry file
- 2 x ⅛" (3 mm) sterling silver oval beads

- 2 white keshi pearl beads
- 4 x 1⅜" (3.5 cm) sterling silver ball pins
- Mandrel
- Plastic-tipped pliers

1. Hold a length of 26-gauge (0.4 mm) sterling silver wire 1½" (4 cm) from one end with a pair of needle-nose pliers. Using your fingers, bend the wire over the jaws at a right angle.

2. Make a loop above the bend of the wire using a pair of round-nose pliers, ending up with the end of wire again at a right angle to the main wire.

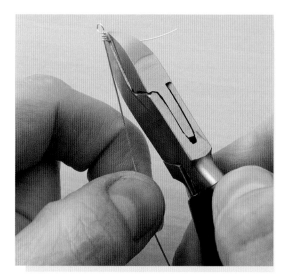

3. With the round-nose pliers slipped through the loop to hold the wire steady, wrap the end of the wire neatly around the main wire four times. Snip off the excess wire close to the wrapped wire. Squeeze the snipped end close to the wrapped wire with a pair of needle-nose pliers.

4. Thread on a ¾" x ⅝" (1.8 x 1.5 cm) amethyst faceted hexagonal crystal bead. Refer to the technique on page 19 (Making a Wrapped Loop) to make a wrapped loop at the other end of the bead, making the loop 1/2" (2 mm) above the bead.

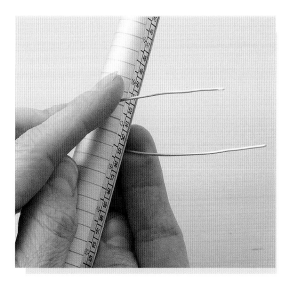

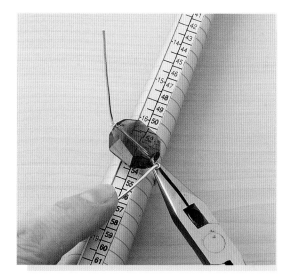

5. File and round the ends of a 6¼" (16 cm) length of 31-gauge (1 mm) sterling silver wire with a jewelry file. Hold the ends of the wire and bend it around a mandrel ⅛" (3 mm) above the size level required.

6. Thread the wrapped loops of the crystal bead onto the wire ends. Slip the bead down the wires to rest against the mandrel at the size level required. Hold the wire below one wrapped loop with a pair of needle-nose pliers. Use your fingers to bend the wire downwards. Repeat to bend the wire above the bead upwards.

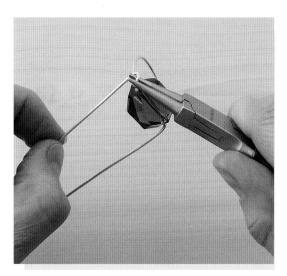

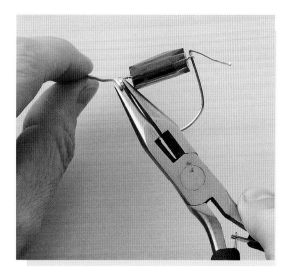

7. Slip the ring off the mandrel. Hold the wire behind the lower wrapped loop with the tips of a pair of round-nose pliers. Wrap the extending wire tightly around the tip until it is pointing upwards.

8. Adjust the jaws of the pliers and bend the wire downwards. Squeeze the coils of the wire together with a pair of needle-nose pliers. Repeat on the other end of the wire.

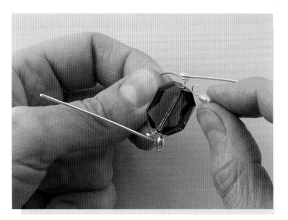

9. Thread two ⅛" (3 mm) sterling silver oval beads and two white keshi pearl beads onto four 1⅜" (3.5 cm) sterling silver ball pins. Refer to the technique on page 18 (Making a Single Loop) to make a single loop above the beads.

10. Open the loops of the silver and pearl beads. Slip a silver bead and a pearl bead onto the wrapped wire at each side of the crystal bead. Close the single loops.

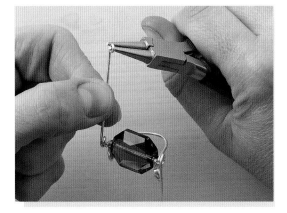

11. Hold the end of the lower wire between the tips of a pair of round-nose pliers. Bend the wire into a circle, facing inwards. Repeat on the upper wire.

12. Holding the circle tightly with a pair of plastic-tipped pliers, coil the wire tightly around one circle. Keep adjusting the grip of the pliers to bend the wire smoothly until you reach the edge of the crystal bead. Repeat on the upper wire.

VARIATION: *Give a ring a southwestern style by using a turquoise bead as the feature bead with a pair of light gold freshwater pearls on ball pins on each side.*

Woven Bead Lariat

A bead loom is a practical device to create a long woven strip of beads. The long length of this sparkling lariat means that it can be worn in various ways and even as a belt. The ends are finished with contrasting colored stripes and a fringe that incorporates bicone crystals. Size 9 rocaille beads are the most versatile size for weaving. It is economical to use quilting thread for this project, as a large amount of thread is needed.

You Will Need

- Quilting thread
- Bead loom
- Water- or air-erasable pen
- Long beading needle
- 10 g (¼ oz) size 9 aquamarine glass rocaille beads
- 80 g (2¾ oz) size 9 silver-lined clear glass rocaille beads
- 28 x ¼" (5 mm) indicolite faceted round crystals
- 42 x ⅛" (4 mm) jet AB bicone crystals

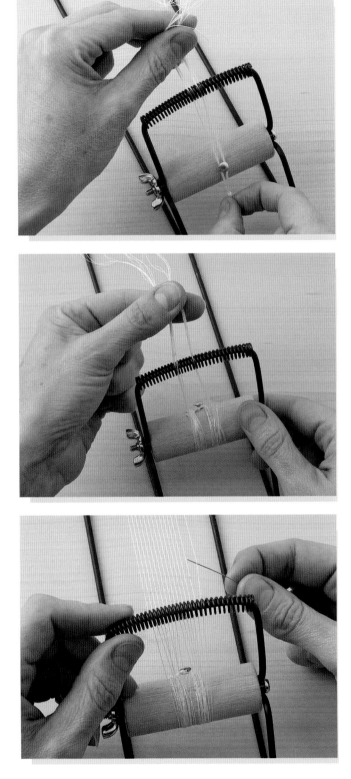

1. Cut fourteen 68" (170 cm) lengths of quilting thread. These are the warp threads that will lay lengthwise in the loom. Tie the threads together with a knot at one end. Lay the threads level and mark them 10" (25 cm) and 54" (135 cm) from the knot with a water- or air-erasable pen. Allow the ink to dry. Divide the bundle in two and slip the knot under the nail head on one of the wooden rollers.

2. Hold the threads taut and turn the roller to wind the warp threads until the pen marks reach the grooves of the metal spring. Tighten the wing nut to hold the roller in place.

3. Position the threads in the grooves of the metal spring, separating the threads with a needle. Turn the loom so that the roller and the metal spring you have been working on is furthest from you. Position the threads in the grooves of the metal spring that is nearest to you, holding the threads taut.

4. Keeping the threads taut, knot the thread ends together. Slip the knot under the nail. Turn the roller to wind the threads around it. Tighten the wing nut to hold the threads taut.

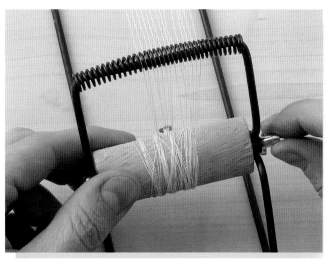

5. Thread a long length of thread onto a long beading needle. This will be the weft thread. Tie the thread to an outside thread close to the pen marks on the roller nearest you, leaving a 6" (15 cm) trailing end of thread. Thread on thirteen size 9 aquamarine glass rocaille beads for the first row and slip them down the weft thread. Position the thread at right angles under the warp threads, then press them up between the warp threads with a finger.

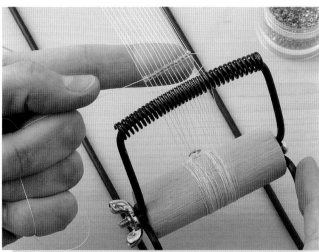

6. Insert the needle back through the beads, making sure that the needle passes above the warp threads to secure the beads in place.

7. Pick up the next row of aquamarine beads and repeat the process. Work a sequence of four rows of aquamarine beads, one row of silver beads, two rows of aquamarine beads, one row of silver beads, two rows of aquamarine beads, two rows of silver beads, one row of aquamarine beads, three rows of silver beads, one row of aquamarine beads, six rows of silver beads, and one row of aquamarine beads. Push the rows of beads together as you work to keep them neat.

8. Continue working rows of silver beads. When you run out of thread, weave the thread back through the rows of beads. Add a new thread as described in Step 5 and continue. When you reach the second roller, loosen the tension on the rollers and roll the beadwork onto the roller to continue until you reach the pen marks on the threads.

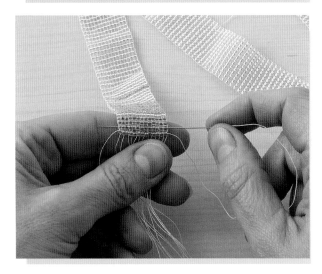

9. Weave one row of aquamarine beads, six rows of silver beads, one row of aquamarine beads, three rows of silver beads, one row of aquamarine beads, two rows of silver beads, two rows of aquamarine beads, one row of silver beads, two rows of aquamarine beads, one row of silver beads, and four rows of aquamarine beads. Loosen the tension on the rollers and remove the work. Cut off the knots. Thread the trailing first weft thread onto a needle. Work the thread back into the work.

10. Starting with the second thread, weave every other thread at the ends of the lariat and the ends of newly joined threads back into the work, leaving seven extending threads for the fringe at each end of the lariat. Cut off the ends of the threads woven back into the beadwork.

11. Thread the first thread onto a needle. To make the fringe, thread on forty aquamarine beads, two ¼" (5 mm) indicolite faceted round crystals, three ⅛" (4 mm) jet AB bicone crystals, and four aquamarine rocaille beads.

12. Insert the needle back through all the beads except the last three rocaille beads and work the thread through the beadwork. Make a fringe of seven hanging beads at each end of the lariat. Cut off the ends of the threads after weaving them back into the beadwork.

VARIATION: *This 27½" (70 cm) lariat is woven with eight threads using blue rocaille beads and sapphire bicone crystals.*

INDEX

Note: Page numbers in **bold** indicate projects. Page numbers in *italics* indicate photos separate from descriptions.